There Is a Harvest *for* Every Season

Discerning What God Is Producing While You Wait

by
Raven Makenzie

Copyright © 2026 by Raven Makenzie Coaching LLC
d/b/a Seed Publications

All rights reserved.

No part of this book may be reproduced, distributed, transmitted, stored in a retrieval system, or shared in any form or by any means - electronic, mechanical, photocopying, recording, or otherwise - without the prior written permission of the author, except for brief quotations used in reviews or scholarly reference.

Scripture quotations are taken from the Holy Bible, New International Version (NIV), unless otherwise noted. All Scripture is quoted for educational and devotional purposes.

This book is intended for inspirational and informational purposes only. It is not a substitute for professional counseling, medical advice, or legal guidance. Readers are encouraged to seek appropriate professional counsel when needed.

Any resemblance to actual persons, living or deceased, or actual events is purely coincidental.

ISBN: 979-8-9921493-1-9

Printed in the United States of America

Table of Contents

Author's Note v
About This Revised Edition.................................. vii
A Seasonal Disclaimer ix
Preface xi
Introduction xiv
Prayer xvi

Part I: Foundations of Seed, Seasons, and Discernment: 1

The Seed and the Harvest 2
The Planting Season 6
No roots, No fruit 11
The Preparation / Rooting Season 15

Part II: Recognizing Seasons & Internal Formation 21

Seasons of Change 22
Seasons of Growth 28
Seasons of Impatience 33
The Waiting Season 38
The Obedience Without Explanation Season 43

Part III: Identity, Silence, and Inner Reconstruction 49

Seasons of Identity Refinement 50

    The Calling Season 55

    The Concealment Season...60

    The Testing Season / Seasons of Silence....................69

Part IV: Strength Under Pressure 75

    Seasons of Lost Hope..76

    Seasons of Learning Faith 83

Part V: Restoration, Healing, and Deliverance.. 89

    Seasons of Rest 90

    Seasons of Deliverance..96

    Seasons of Healing...102

Part VI: Fruit, Stewardship, and Multiplication ..109

    The Harvest Season..110

    Seasons of Love 116

    The Governing Season 125

    The Maintenance Season 129

    The Multiplication Season......................................134

Part VII: Completion & Commissioning...........139

    The Completion / Transition Season 140

    A Harvest for Every Season....................................145

    About the Author 150

Author's Note

This book was written from lived obedience, not theory.

When I first wrote *A Harvest for Every Season*, I was learning, often in real time, how God works through seasons of planting, waiting, pruning, and harvest. What began as personal revelation became a shared language for many who were trying to make sense of God's timing in their own lives.

Over time, as I walked with others through seasons of loss, transition, healing, and growth, I realized something important: people were not struggling because they lacked faith. They were struggling because they did not know what season they were in, and therefore did not know how to respond wisely.

Scripture is clear: God is not random. He is orderly, intentional, and faithful. He works through seasons, and each season carries both an assignment and a promise.

This expanded & revised edition exists to bring clarity where there was confusion, language where there was silence, and peace where there was unnecessary striving.

"To everything there is a season, and a time for every purpose under heaven." **—Ecclesiastes 3:1**

Raven Makenzie

About This Revised Edition

This Revised & Expanded Edition of *A Harvest for Every Season* preserves the heart, testimony, and foundational teachings of the original work while offering additional clarity, structure, and discernment for the reader.

The original chapters remain intact and honored. New chapters have been added to name and explain seasons that were previously experienced but not always clearly defined, such as calling, concealment, stewardship, and multiplication.

Each season in this edition is framed with three guiding questions: What is God doing in this season? What is my responsibility here? What kind of harvest does this season prepare me for?

This edition is designed to be both pastoral and practical; a resource for reflection, prayer, discernment, and growth.

"Let us not grow weary while doing good, for in due season we shall reap if we do not lose heart."
— **Galatians 6:9**

A Seasonal Disclaimer

This book is intended to guide discernment, not replace it.

The seasons described in *There is A Harvest for Every Season* are not rigid stages, formulas, or timelines. They are biblical patterns meant to help you recognize how God often works, not rules that confine how He must work.

Seasons may overlap. Some may repeat. Others may be experienced simultaneously in different areas of life.

Discernment is not mechanical. It is relational.

"My sheep hear My voice, and I know them, and they follow Me." — **John 10:27**

This book is not meant to encourage passivity, delay obedience, or justify inaction under the label of waiting.

If at any point you feel anxious, rushed, or burdened by interpretation, pause. Peace is often the first sign of alignment.

"Trust in the Lord with all your heart, and lean not on your own understanding." — **Proverbs 3:5**

Preface

Life is not lived in straight lines.

It is lived in cycles, seedtime and harvest, preparation and pruning, waiting and fulfillment, loss and restoration. Yet many of us were never taught how to discern the seasons we are in, let alone how to steward them well. As a result, we often grow weary, confused, or discouraged when life does not unfold the way we expected.

This book was written to restore clarity.

There Is a Harvest for Every Season is not a promise that every season will feel good, easy, or productive by worldly standards. It is a declaration that no season is wasted, and that every season, when rightly understood, produces fruit. Some harvests are visible. Others are internal. Some are immediate. Others mature quietly over time. But all are intentional.

Scripture teaches us that God works through process. He establishes roots before fruit, character before calling, and endurance before expansion. The Kingdom does not reward haste, it honors faithfulness. This book is structured around that truth, offering a framework for recognizing seasons not as interruptions to your life, but as instruments of formation within it.

Each chapter explores a distinct season that believers commonly experience; growth, waiting, testing, love, maintenance, rest, identity, multiplication, and more. These are not linear stages that we "graduate" from once and for all, but recurring rhythms we will encounter again and again throughout our lives. The goal is not to escape seasons quickly, but to discern them accurately and harvest them fully.

Throughout this book, you will be invited to do more than read. You will be asked to reflect, examine, and respond. Each season carries an assignment, because seasons are not passive experiences; they are invitations to partner with God in the work He is doing within you. When seasons are misunderstood, they can feel like punishment. When they are discerned rightly, they become preparation.

This book is written for those who have felt stuck, delayed, or disoriented. For those who have wondered why obedience did not immediately produce results. For those who are tempted to abandon the process because the fruit has not yet appeared. And for those who are learning, sometimes painfully, that harvest is not the end of the work, but the beginning of greater responsibility.

Above all, this book is an invitation to trust the God of the process. There is a harvest in your season! Yes, even this one. The question is not *if* God is producing fruit. The question is whether you will stay long enough to reap it.

Introduction

It is not every day that we recognize the beauty of the seasons we are living through. As people born into sin, we are often more attuned to loss than to gain, more aware of discomfort than of purpose. When circumstances shift, our instinct is to focus on what is being taken from us rather than what is being formed within us. In seasons of storms, testing, or trial, we can become so consumed by the difficulty of the moment that we miss God entirely. But that perspective is about to change. This book was placed on my heart to reveal a truth that reshaped the way I understand life, faith, and process: there is a harvest for every season.

In 2018, I was sitting on my living room couch binge-watching sermons from a few of my favorite pastors. Over and over again, I heard the same phrase echoed from different pulpits: "In due season, you will reap a harvest." There is nothing wrong with that teaching. Scripture affirms it clearly: "Let us not grow weary in doing good, for in due season we shall reap, if we do not faint" (Galatians 6:9). But in that quiet moment, as I listened, the Holy Spirit spoke something deeper to my heart: every season has a harvest. That revelation shifted my perspective permanently.

If we are not careful, we can interpret that scripture to mean that only certain seasons are productive, and that we must endure barren ones while waiting for a future payoff. But Scripture does not teach delayed fruitfulness, it teaches continual opportunity. Every season carries something to be gathered, something to be learned, something to be reaped. Due season does not mean a distant moment we passively wait for; it means the appointed time reached by endurance. The prerequisite is not perfection; it's perseverance. We reap not by escaping the season, but by remaining faithful within it.

This book was written to illuminate the seasons I believe every believer will face; seasons of planting, waiting, testing, silence, pruning, growth, rest, love, and renewal, and to reveal the harvest hidden within each one. Not all harvests are tangible. Some strengthen your faith. Some refine your character. Some deepen your discernment. And some prepare you to carry what is coming next.

Every season has a harvest. But only hearts anchored in God will recognize what is being produced, and only those who do not faint will gather it.

Prayer

Heavenly Father,

It is with gladness in my heart that I write these words before you, that these your people will be blessed from the word that you gave me, that every season has a harvest, Lord. I pray that you open up their hearts and their minds to receive from you God as you use me to express your thoughts and ideas on the pages of this book. I pray that you silence the naysayers- that those who have spoken against your people will have front row seats to the glory that you will get through their lives and through their obedience. God, I pray that any hindering or distracting spirit be silenced now in the name of Jesus, so that the reader can fully receive from you Lord. Let your will be done in each and every one of their lives, in Jesus name. Father I thank you, I bless you, I give you all the glory. In Jesus name I pray and give thanks. Amen

PART I:

Foundations of Seed, Seasons, and Discernment

Understanding how God works before we interpret what He's doing. *"First the blade, then the ear, then the full grain in the ear."* —**Mark 4:28**

The Seed and the Harvest

Every harvest follows a seed, and every seed reveals alignment. What we reap in life is never accidental; it is always the result of what was sown, where it was planted, and why it was released. This is not merely an agricultural principle; it is a spiritual law that governs every area of life.

Scripture establishes this order plainly: "While the earth remains, seedtime and harvest... shall not cease" (Genesis 8:22). As long as life continues, this rhythm remains intact. No season is exempt. No moment is neutral. Seedtime and harvest are always at work.

So before asking what you are believing God for, the better question is why. Are your desires rooted in God's will, or in the appetites of the flesh? This distinction matters, because a life oriented toward self cannot fully participate in the harvest God intends. If we only pursue what benefits us naturally, we will miss the deeper abundance God is forming within us spiritually.

Harvest does not begin when something appears in your hands, it begins when something is established in your spirit. Reaping, receiving, and increase are first birthed inwardly before they are ever reflected outwardly. Nothing sustainable can manifest in the natural that has not already taken root in the spiritual. If this is true of creation itself, how much more is it true of the harvests we seek from God? Every season is sowing something, whether we are aware of it or not.

God's design is intentional. He fills us in the Spirit so that we can pour out in the natural. He develops us inwardly so that fruit can endure outward pressure. The seed and the harvest are not simply about God blessing you, they are about God forming you into someone who can carry blessing without losing alignment. Harvest is God giving you what you need so that His glory can be sown in your life and multiplied through it across the earth.

Up to this point, it would be comforting to believe that harvest is automatic, detached from our choices, habits, and posture. But Scripture removes that illusion with sobering clarity:

"Do not be deceived: God is not mocked, for whatever one sows, that will he also reap" — **Galatians 6:7**.

This verse is not a threat; it is a revelation. Harvest is honest. It reflects what has truly been planted, not merely what was intended, hoped for, or prayed about. Self-deception is one of the greatest dangers in seedtime, because we can convince ourselves that we are sowing one thing while consistently planting another.

God is not mocked. Not because He is harsh, but because His laws are faithful. Seedtime and harvest do not bend to emotion, urgency, or impatience. They respond to alignment. What we repeatedly sow in thought, word, behavior, devotion, and discipline will eventually surface. Harvest exposes what was actually planted beneath the surface.

This is why spiritual harvest must come first. If the soil of the heart is neglected, no amount of outward effort will produce lasting fruit. If the seed is misaligned, the harvest will disappoint, no matter how sincerely we prayed for it, and this brings us to a truth we cannot ignore.

Harvest is never disconnected from depth. Fruit does not appear where roots have not been allowed to grow. What we see above ground is always dependent on what has been cultivated below it. Many people desire the fruit of peace without the root of trust, the fruit of discipline without the root of obedience, the fruit of love without the root of surrender, and the fruit of endurance without the root of perseverance. But, God's design does not work that way. Seedtime determines fruit, but roots determine survival. Before fruit can be sustained, roots must be established. Because in the Kingdom, there is no shortcut to maturity. There is no fruit without formation, and there is no harvest where roots were never allowed to grow. No roots. No fruit.

The Planting Season

"Sow your seed in the morning and keep busy all afternoon, for you do not know if profit will come from one activity or another - or maybe both." — **Ecclesiastes 11:6**

I have spent many years sowing and reaping; into gardens, into people, into places, and one truth has proven consistent in every environment: if you want a harvest, seed must first go into the ground.

A farmer is never afraid to let the seed in his hand go. He gives it freely into the soil, trusting that in due season the ground will multiply and return what he has given. If he did not trust the soil, he would never plant at all, and without planting, there would be no harvest. The irony is this: The abundance he hopes for is already in his hands, housed within the seed. However, it can only be unlocked by surrender. Many individuals are in this position - carrying the answer to their prayers for increase nestled in the palm of their hands, but they're too afraid to plant the seed out of fear that the seed won't multiply.

The farmer understands that what he sows in seed form is always less than what he will reap. He plants without knowing the exact yield, but with full confidence that a yield *will* come. In that sense, he sows blindly, not in ignorance, but in faith. He understands that planting requires faith because sowing always precedes seeing. And that is why this season often feels slow, costly, and unrewarded. It's not easy to give out of lack, but building a life out of lack is harder.

Faithfulness now determines fruitfulness later. No matter who you are, if you look at your life, this exact moment is a direct harvest of everything you've planted. On the flipside, it's also a direct reflection of everything you *didn't* sow. I cover this topic in great detail in my book, *Wisdom from Eden.* It's a valuable resource for anyone who endeavors to learn the secrets of multiplicity. This chapter will focus not only on the principles of sowing, but the frequency in which you sow.

In January of 2026, the Lord confronted my understanding of harvest in a way I did not expect. By that point, I had written two books on sowing and reaping, articulating the principle with confidence and clarity. Yet my daily life revealed a quieter truth: I believed the revelation enough to teach it, but not yet enough to live it without reserve.

The challenge came not only to me, but to my husband and me together. The Lord spoke plainly: "I want you to give five hundred dollars a month, until I do it." We knew immediately what *until I do it* meant. We had been praying for increase. Yet we were standing in the middle of contradiction, facing a second eviction just three months after moving into our new home, carrying over one hundred and fifty thousand dollars in debt, and struggling to afford even groceries and gas.

When the Lord answered our prayers with a call to give, the weight of the moment became clear. Give...until I do it revealed two undeniable truths. First, the harvest was already finished in heaven. Second, its manifestation in the earth was tethered to our obedience. This was not a lesson in generosity. It was an invitation into alignment, where faith is proven, not proclaimed, and where harvest responds to seed.

We knew how costly obedience would be. We were intimately aware of our lack; what we did not yet know was the increase God had already prepared for us. Faith does not struggle with what is visible, it wrestles with what is unseen. And this instruction forced us to stand between the two.

The test was not simply the amount. The test was the absence of instruction. The Lord did not tell us who to give to, only that we were to give five hundred dollars every single month until He did it. There was no timeline. No marker for completion. No defined end. Only sustained obedience, anchored in trust rather than certainty. This is where faith is purified. Because when obedience has no expiration date, it can no longer be negotiated. It becomes posture.

I already know that when the Lord does what He has promised, the giving will not decrease, it will be challenged to increase. Harvest always demands greater capacity, and God prepares that capacity through obedience long before abundance arrives. The revelation in all of this is simple, yet costly: God was not asking us to give according to our present condition. He was asking us to give according to what was already finished. Heaven was not waiting on our provision, our provision was waiting on alignment. God does not command what He has not already supplied. He does not ask for seed that He has not already placed within the hands of the sower. If He called us to give it, then it already existed, whether we could see it yet or not.

This is what a true planting season looks like. It rarely feels productive. It often feels hidden, unrewarded, and misunderstood. There is no immediate applause for seed in the ground, only dirt, pressure, and patience. From the outside, it can appear as sacrifice without recognition, or obedience without evidence. Yet in the unseen, vineyard upon vineyard is being established, harvest layered upon harvest long before a single fruit breaks the surface.

Planting seasons are not designed to validate you; they are designed to anchor you. The work of this season is not to see the harvest, but to stay postured to sow. Faith here is measured by consistency, not outcome. Progress is no longer calculated by visible return, but by unwavering obedience. You are not behind because nothing appears to be happening. You are ahead because something eternal is being formed beneath the soil.

The assignment of this season is simple, but not easy: sow without keeping score. Give without negotiating results. Remain faithful without demanding proof. Because when God marks a season for planting, He is not delaying harvest, He is multiplying it. Sow faithfully. Sow continually. Reap abundantly.

Potential Harvest

Planting produces:
- Increase
- Multiplication
- Provision in later seasons

No roots, No fruit

We must first recognize this foundational truth: a pure harvest cannot come from an unestablished root system. Nothing honorable, lasting, or fruitful can grow if nothing of substance has been planted and allowed to take root. Every season you walk through, no matter how quiet, slow, or confusing, carries a harvest within it. But that harvest is determined by what has been developing beneath the surface. Scripture gives us a clear picture of this principle:

> *"You're a tree planted in Eden, bearing fresh fruit every month, never dropping a leaf, always in blossom."*
> **— Psalm 1:3 (MSG)**

Psalm 1 tells us that the righteous bear fruit in every season. Not because circumstances are always favorable, but because their roots are firmly planted. We are able to live righteously because we are the harvest of God's seed. Christ planted His life in us, and as we remain connected to Him, the fruit of the Spirit is continually produced. The longer we walk with Jesus, the more our lives should resemble His. Growth is expected, but growth is never instant. Nothing living grows overnight.

If you feel stagnant, frustrated, or unfruitful, the question is not whether God is working, it is whether you are remaining connected to the source. We have already identified the seed as Jesus and the harvest as the fruit of the Spirit. Now we must understand the process that connects the two: roots. Jesus makes this unmistakably clear:

> *"Remain in me, as I also remain in you. No branch can bear fruit by itself; it must remain in the vine... apart from me you can do nothing."* — **John 15:4-5 (NIV)**

That final phrase carries sobering weight: apart from me you can do nothing. Fruit does not grow independently. Roses do not grow apart from rosebushes. Grapes do not grow apart from the vine. In the same way, spiritual fruit cannot be sustained without spiritual connection. This is not about proximity, it is about dependence. Roots are formed through remaining.

I learned this lesson early, without realizing it at the time. In second grade, my teacher assigned us a project to grow flowers in small plastic cups placed on the classroom windowsill. We were given soil, seeds, water, and instructions. I followed them carefully. I planted the seed, watered it diligently, and moved my cup to follow the sunlight each day. I was intentional. I was hopeful. But after weeks passed with no visible growth, my excitement turned into disappointment. I became convinced that nothing was happening. One day, overwhelmed by impatience, I dumped the soil out of my cup, and to my surprise, the seed had sprouted.

Beneath the surface, roots had formed and filled the bottom of the cup. Panicked, I rushed to put everything back, watered it excessively, and returned it to the windowsill. But it never recovered. While my classmates' plants eventually broke through the soil, mine did not. I had destroyed it by disrupting what was developing underground. I didn't understand then that growth has an order. I didn't understand that roots come before fruit. By overturning the foundation, I killed what was actually alive. Sadly, this is often how we treat our spiritual lives.

We assume nothing is happening because nothing is visible. We dig, rush, compare, and interfere with what God is quietly establishing. But just because you cannot see growth does not mean growth is absent. The most critical work often happens where the eye cannot reach. God grows foundations before He produces fruit.

The things you cannot see, character, endurance, trust, discipline, humility, become the support system for what you eventually can see. Without roots, fruit cannot survive. Without depth, growth collapses under pressure. Scripture affirms this clearly:

> *"So then, just as you received Christ Jesus as Lord, continue to live your lives in Him, rooted and built up in Him, strengthened in the faith as you were taught, and overflowing with thankfulness."* — **Colossians 2:6–7**

Roots are not optional. They are essential. They anchor identity, stabilize growth, and determine longevity. Fruit may attract attention, but roots determine whether that fruit can remain. And this is the truth that carries us forward: There can be no lasting harvest where roots were never allowed to grow.

The Preparation / Rooting Season

"Other seed fell on good soil and yielded a crop."
— **Luke 8:8**

Before fruit appears above ground, roots must deepen below it. I often tell the people I coach and minister to that the preparation season is not something we wait to enter, it is something we are always in. Preparation is always *now*. Whether we recognize it or not, the present moment is shaping us for what comes next. What you prepared for ten years ago may be what sustains you tomorrow. What you prepare for today may be what you need tonight. There is no wasted season when preparation is stewarded with intention.

Scripture gives us a clear picture of the depth of this posture in the life of Joseph. When God revealed that a famine was coming to the land, Joseph did not wait for the crisis to arrive before responding. His heart was for God, and subsequently for God's people, and that posture shaped how he responded to the revelation regarding the famine: He utilized his current position to steward the present season of abundance in preparation for what God had revealed. His preparation was not reactive. Not in the sense that he waited for famine to hit before responding. Instead, it was intentional and continual, and because Joseph honored the present moment, an entire nation was preserved. Joseph understood that revelation without preparation saves no one, but revelation with preparation is partnership with God.

This is the rhythm of God's design; to be postured actively and continually in preparation. Every day is an opportunity to prepare for the next. Yesterday's obedience becomes tomorrow's authority. Single seasons prepare us for marriage. Student seasons prepare us for leadership. Learning seasons prepare us for discipleship, so on, and so forth. No matter how we look at it, the ground we walk today becomes the platform we stand on tomorrow. Every season carries within it the seeds of the next, if we are attentive enough to tend them well. You must realize preparation is not a phase we graduate from, it is a posture we maintain. What we do or don't do now, determines how prepared or unprepared we are for what is next. As Scripture reminds us, we are to be "rooted and built up in Him, strengthened in the faith" (Colossians 2:7). Preparation always precedes position.

Preparation seasons may go unnoticed by others, because they establish stability long before fruit appears. But, what is formed here determines whether what grows later can endure. These seasons are quiet, unseen, and often undervalued, yet they determine the strength of everything that follows from your life. This is the season many people often want to skip because, as mentioned earlier, nothing visible seems to be happening. There are no announcements, no measurable progress, and no outward confirmation. Yet, this is where the future of the harvest is decided. This is the season where God builds what applause cannot sustain.

Jesus makes it clear that fruitfulness is not primarily about opportunity, gifting, or exposure, but about depth. The difference between seed that survives and seed that withers is not intention, but soil. In fact, the fruit is simply the default response to good soil, and from the abundance of it brings forth opportunities to give, expand, and multiply. Good soil, though, is not accidental, or standard across the board; it is cultivated. In the preparation season, God tends the soil of the heart, where motives are purified, desires are refined, and weak roots are exposed and strengthened.

What cannot yet survive pressure is quietly reinforced before it is ever asked to produce. This is why preparation often feels like an exaggerated or elongated season: Roots must grow downward before anything grows outward.

In this season, God is not trying to impress anyone; He is trying to establish you. What is formed here will determine how you handle pressure later. Shallow roots collapse under weight, but deep roots hold steady through storms. Preparation seasons are marked by obscurity, repetition, and obedience without visibility. They teach you how to remain faithful without affirmation and anchored when no one is watching. This is where calling is clarified and character is formed. The world rewards visibility, but God rewards depth.

Sadly, many people often confuse invisibility with insignificance, but Scripture consistently affirms that what God builds in secret carries public consequence. What is formed quietly becomes what sustains you when fruit appears. If God rushed fruit before roots were ready, the result would not be abundance, it would be collapse. So He delays visibility to ensure stability. He allows the work to remain hidden so that when exposure comes, it does not destroy what He has built. This season protects you from premature fruit your foundation cannot yet support.

Your assignment while in the preparation season is not to perform, but to grow privately. This is the season to strengthen foundations, deepen your relationship with God, and practice obedience without recognition. This is the season to develop discipline, consistency, and reverence for process, to say yes when no one applauds, to remain faithful when nothing is visible, and to trust that God sees what is being formed beneath the surface. Preparation seasons may not feel productive, but they are essential. They determine whether fruit will last or fail under pressure. What God establishes in this season may go unnoticed by people, but it will be unshakable when fruit finally appears. Roots come first. And because they do, fruit will follow.

Potential Harvest

This season produces:
- Endurance
- Stability
- Spiritual maturity
- Emotional depth

PART II:

Recognizing Seasons & Internal Formation

How God develops us internally before anything changes externally. *"Be transformed by the renewing of your mind."* — **Romans 12:2**

Seasons of Change

Change is the one constant present in every season of life. It is uncomfortable, often unwelcome, and frequently misunderstood, yet it is unavoidable. In fact, change is the very marker by which seasons are identified. Without change, there would be no distinction between one season and the next.

When I asked the Lord how this book should be structured, He made one thing clear: understanding seasons requires understanding change. Before we can recognize harvest, we must learn how to discern transition. Change is not a sign that God has left, it is often the sign that He is working.

We identify natural seasons by observable shifts. Leaves change color and fall. Temperatures rise and drop. Light shortens and lengthens. Even without a calendar, we would still know the season by what is changing around us. In the same way, spiritual seasons are discerned by internal and external shifts, new responsibilities, altered desires, disrupted routines, unexpected doors opening or closing. When change appears, wisdom asks God not why first, but what season am I in?

We tend to tolerate change when it aligns with our expectations. But sudden or disruptive change often produces resistance. A new job schedule, loss of employment, pregnancy, relocation, added responsibility, or unexpected limitation can provoke fear, frustration, or grief. Yet when we look back, we often see that God's hand was present, even when the transition felt unwanted. Scripture reminds us that change is not random:

> *"Do not be deceived: God is not mocked. Whatever one sows, that will he also reap."* — **Galatians 6:7**

This verse reveals an important truth: some change is the result of seeds we planted, intentionally or unintentionally. Other change arrives because God ordained a shift independent of our choosing. Both require discernment. Both require endurance.

I learned this through one of the most defining changes of my life. At nineteen years old, I discovered I was pregnant. I was a college dropout with big dreams and little stability, and the news sent me into deep depression. Fear spoke louder than faith. Shame distorted my identity. The enemy whispered lies about my worth, my future, my body, and my ability to be loved. In my mind, abortion felt like the only escape.

When my mother discovered the pregnancy, she drew a clear boundary. If I went through with the abortion, I would not have her support. I found myself weighing impossible options; losing my mother or losing my child. As I walked into the abortion clinic, I was met by believers praying outside, quietly worshiping, handing me a pamphlet that read, Jesus saves. That phrase would not leave my spirit. I did not go through with the abortion.

In time, I came to understand something crucial: God was not punishing me. I was reaping the result of a decision, but God redeemed the outcome. My daughter was the harvest of a seed I planted, but she also became the seed God used to save my life. Through her, my family was restored, my heart was softened, and my journey toward Christ accelerated. What felt like devastation became deliverance. What felt like loss became legacy. This is the mystery of change.

Some seasons shift because of our actions. Others shift because God has set them on a fixed course. Scripture tells us that God created the sun, moon, and stars to mark seasons, days, and years (Genesis 1:14–15). Change, therefore, is not chaos, it is order.

We often misunderstand harvest because we define it too narrowly. We celebrate visible abundance and overlook internal formation. We praise spring and despise winter, forgetting that winter prepares the soil for what spring reveals. Scripture corrects our vision:

"We look not to the things that are seen but to the things that are unseen. For what is seen is temporary, but what is unseen is eternal." — **2 Corinthians 4:18**

Not all harvests are tangible. Some seasons harvest wisdom. Others harvest humility, discernment, self-control, patience, or intimacy with God. Change itself can be the harvest, because it moves us from who we were into who God is forming us to be.

Spring illustrates this perfectly. While it represents life and new beginnings, it also brings discomfort, pollen, insects, rain, disrupted rhythms. There is beauty, but there is also resistance. No rain, no flowers. No endurance, no harvest. The same is true spiritually. We must endure change to reap its reward. Seeds require darkness and light. They must be planted, and buried, before they can rise. Planted does not mean abandoned. Darkness is not rejection; it is preparation.

"When you sow a seed, it does not come to life unless it dies." — **1 Corinthians 15:37**

Change marks the end of one form and the beginning of another. The seed cannot remain a seed forever. Growth demands transition.

And here is what we must not miss: the harvest is not just for the seed. Roots provide stability. Depth produces endurance. Height brings visibility. Fruit enables multiplication. What God grows in you through change is meant to nourish others as well. So do not despise change. Do not quit in transition. Do not misinterpret discomfort as absence. Change may be the very harvest you prayed for, just not in the form you expected. Endure. Remain rooted. Do not faint. Change is coming again, and this time, you will recognize what you are sowing. This time, you will recognize the harvest.

The assignment of the season of change is discernment, endurance, and surrender. This season requires you to resist reacting impulsively to discomfort and instead remain attentive to what God is forming. Change exposes what you rely on, what you fear losing, and where you are tempted to control outcomes rather than trust God's process. The work of this season is not to escape transition, but to submit to it without bitterness, panic, or withdrawal.

Change often removes familiar structures before new ones are revealed. The assignment is to stay rooted in God while everything else shifts. When you remain faithful in transition, change becomes a tool of formation rather than a source of fear.

Possible Harvests:

- Discernment
- Self-control
- Trust
- Spiritual maturity

Not every harvest can be held in your hands. Some harvests shape who you are becoming.

Seasons of Growth

Growing pains are never comfortable. But growth is inevitable once seeds have been sown. As a result of obedience, surrender, and alignment, what has been planted will eventually be fertilized, initiating growth. Like change, growth is not a one-time experience; it is a recurring season we encounter again and again throughout our walk with God.

God does not allow us to remain who we were before we met Him. Yet He is patient in how He develops us. Growth happens gradually. As we grow, certain people, habits, comforts, and even versions of ourselves must fall away. Some parts of you simply cannot go where God is taking you. Anything that would hinder your development must be removed. Scripture calls this pruning, and it is essential in seasons of growth.

> *"I am the true vine, and My Father is the vinedresser. Every branch in Me that does not bear fruit He takes*

away, and every branch that does bear fruit He prunes, that it may bear more fruit." — **John 15:1-2**

Pruning is not optional. It is evidence that growth is occurring. Without pruning, what should flourish becomes entangled and eventually collapses.

I learned this through something as simple as a rose bush. One spring, my rose bushes bloomed beautifully after a long winter. But because I failed to tend them properly, a thorny vine grew up from the ground and wrapped itself tightly around the branches. It choked the life out of the roses and grew so heavy that the entire bush fell over. The only solution was to cut everything down and remove the vine at the root.

That thorny vine is a picture of what happens when unhealthy relationships, unforgiveness, distractions, habits, and influences are allowed to grow unchecked. They intertwine with our calling, restrict our growth, and eventually overwhelm us. Pruning prevents collapse. Loss in a growth season is often mercy, not punishment.

The same principle applies to human development. What once worked will eventually stop working. Just as a child must outgrow dependence in order to mature, believers must move beyond earlier stages of faith. What was once acceptable becomes insufficient. This transition can feel painful, confusing, and even unfair, but it is necessary.

In 2018, I entered a season of growth unlike any I had experienced before. God woke me one morning and said, "I see you're ready to know who you are." From that moment forward, He began revealing my call and purpose. This growth began with pruning.

First, people were removed, some I had known for over fourteen plus years. God made it clear they would become hindrances later. Then my appetites changed. Music, conversations, and environments I once tolerated became unbearable. Finally, God dealt with my habits, attitude, and inner life.

He instructed me to walk through my home and see it as a reflection of myself. My bedroom represented my mind; cluttered, chaotic, disordered. My bathrooms represented my mouth; clean on the surface, but filthy in hidden places. My kitchen represented my heart; empty, cold, undecorated, lifeless. Through cleaning and restoring those spaces, God revealed the internal work He was doing in me.

As I brought order to my room, my thinking changed.

"Let God transform you into a new person by changing the way you think." — **Romans 12:2**

As my thinking changed, my speech followed.

"Let no unwholesome talk come out of your mouths..."
— **Ephesians 4:29**

And finally, God dealt with my heart, the place I had guarded the most. Growth required facing buried pain, uprooting old wounds, and allowing warmth where coldness had lived. Only then could real fruit begin to grow.

I later realized that I had asked God to prune me. Growth hurt because it required honesty, surrender, and responsibility. God showed me who I was so I could become who He had already declared me to be.

"If anyone is in Christ, he is a new creation... the old has passed away, the new has come." — **2 Corinthians 5:17**

Growth is painful, but it is necessary. Growth is not punishment. It is preparation. Instead of asking, "Why is this happening to me?" the better question is, "What is this happening for?" Pain in growth seasons stretches us beyond comfort so we can become dependent on God rather than on what once sustained us. And here is where growth naturally leads into the next season: waiting.

Growth often outpaces visibility. Roots deepen before fruit appears. After pruning, after stretching, after surrender, there is often a pause; a season where nothing seems to be happening outwardly. But waiting is not stagnation.

Waiting is where growth settles, strengthens, and prepares for fruit.

The assignment of the growth season is submission, cooperation, and perseverance. This season requires you to allow God to remove what no longer fits, without clinging to familiarity. Growth demands humility, the willingness to be reshaped, corrected, and refined without retreating. You are called to endure discomfort without abandoning obedience and to trust that pruning is producing capacity, not loss. Growth is not about speed. It is about readiness. Growth prepares you for fruit, but it also prepares you for waiting, the season where roots hold firm, faith is tested, and patience completes its work. Because what grows too fast cannot last.

Possible Harvests:

- Goodness
- Spiritual maturity
- Inner order
- Capacity

Seasons of Impatience

Here is where things get uncomfortable, and honest. You have fertilized a seed. You have carried it for weeks, months, maybe even years. For some, it is a business, a ministry, a nonprofit, a book, a family, a calling, or a vision God whispered to you long ago. You know something is alive inside of you, yet you cannot touch it. You cannot present it. You cannot release it. You can only carry it, and carrying, over time, creates pressure.

Whether you are trying to push through the soil or move through the birthing canal, one truth remains: birth requires endurance. There comes a moment when the only instruction is to P.U.S.H.; pray until something happens. But pushing too early can be just as dangerous as refusing to push at all.

A person can be in labor and not yet be ready to deliver. Dilation may be happening, pressure may be increasing, but timing still matters. Much of impatience comes from being able to see growth without being able to hold the outcome. Other times, impatience comes from our demand for immediacy. We are accustomed to asking and receiving, so when the answer is "not yet," we assume it means "never." But delay is not denial. Delay is often protection.

A vision must be birthed fully in order to be stewarded correctly. An idea imagined is far easier than a calling lived. God does not release prematurely what we are not yet equipped to sustain. Sometimes the delay is not about the vision, it is about the vessel. Instead of asking, Why is this happening to me? this season invites better questions:

1. Where does my impatience come from?
2. What is God forming in me right now?
3. What would break if this manifested too soon?

"To everything there is a season, and a time for every purpose under heaven." — **Ecclesiastes 3:1**

God's timing is perfect, even when it conflicts with our urgency. Anxiety does not accelerate divine appointments. Pressure does not force God's hand. If we are not centered, what we produce will not reflect Him. We were created to create, but only in alignment with the Creator. I learned this the hard way.

When God first called me to ministry, He showed me a vision of preaching the gospel to thousands. I did not yet understand what He was revealing, but I did not allow my lack of understanding to slow me down. Instead, I tried to force the vision. I organized events, led studies without grounding, and spoke without preparation. I was out of season and underdeveloped.

The result was stress, confusion, and discouragement. I blamed God for what failed, not realizing I had rushed what was never assigned to that season. I needed to learn that it's okay to carry the revelation without rushing its fulfillment. God showed me the destination, not the departure time. The vision was given to anchor my hope, not to trigger my impatience.

> *"For I know the plans I have for you… plans to give you a future and a hope."* — **Jeremiah 29:11**

God shows us what will be so we can endure what is. He reveals the what long before the when. Some of you were shown family before healing, leadership before maturity, influence before formation. God did not reveal these things to frustrate you, He revealed them to keep you faithful while He prepares you.

> *"For a thousand years in Your sight are like a day that has just gone by."* — **Psalm 90:4**

I once heard an illustration that brought this season into sharp focus. A plane sat on a runway, fully designed to fly, yet delayed. Unaware of the true circumstances, impatience grew, because to the passenger, it should have been in the air. But, had it taken off before every system was cleared, lives would have been lost. Function must match design before elevation is permitted, and the same is true for us.

If God has you waiting, something is still being calibrated. Something unseen is being secured. Seasons of impatience are not about punishment, they are about formation.

The assignment of this season is to learn restraint without resentment and trust without timelines. This is the season where God invites you to remain submitted when everything in you wants to rush ahead. You are called to guard your heart from comparison, frustration, and self-imposed deadlines, and to resist the temptation to force doors that God has not yet opened. Impatience tests whether you will honor God's process as much as His promise.

In this season, faith is expressed not through movement, but through stillness, choosing obedience when progress feels slow, choosing gratitude when outcomes are delayed, and choosing alignment over acceleration. What you protect here is not the vision itself, but your posture toward God while you wait. Those who complete this season well do not emerge empty-handed; they emerge fortified, steady, and prepared to steward what is coming without breaking under its weight. Impatience does not mean you are out of alignment, it often means you are standing at the threshold of waiting. These seasons walk together, shaping not just what you receive, but who you become while you wait.

Possible Harvests

- Patience
- Self-control
- Discernment
- Emotional maturity
- Deeper trust in God's faithfulness

The Waiting Season

Waiting is not inactivity, it is alignment. It is the season that often follows impatience, not as correction, but as completion. After the tension of desire and the ache of delay, waiting teaches us how to remain steady without forcing movement. This is the space where God slows our hands so He can strengthen our trust, where timing becomes more important than talent, and obedience outweighs urgency. Waiting does not mean nothing is happening; it means something deeper is being formed. In this season, God is not withholding the promise; He is preparing the vessel that will receive it. What feels like delay is often protection, and what feels like silence is frequently instruction.

Waiting exposes what we believe about God when results are postponed. Do we still trust His goodness when progress is invisible? Do we still obey when there is no confirmation that anything is changing? Scripture makes it clear that waiting has always been central to God's design. Abraham waited decades for Isaac. Joseph waited through betrayal and imprisonment. David was anointed king and sent back to the field. In each case, the waiting was not wasted, it was essential. God was not only preparing the promise; He was preparing the person who would steward it.

> *"Wait for the Lord; be strong, and let your heart take courage; wait for the Lord."* — **Psalm 27:14**

Waiting strengthens the inner man. It builds endurance where impatience would have produced collapse. This season develops discernment, humility, emotional stability, and restraint. It trains us to move only when God moves, to speak only when He speaks, and to trust that delay does not mean denial. One of the greatest dangers in this season is attempting to manufacture outcomes. When we rush what God is still forming, we often receive something prematurely and then struggle to sustain it. Waiting protects us from premature exposure and misplaced responsibility.

> *"But they who wait for the Lord shall renew their strength; they shall mount up with wings like eagles..."*
> — **Isaiah 40:31**

I understand this season so intimately, as I lived it for nearly a decade. In 2014, just after I gave my life to Christ, I was in a relationship I should not have been in. My heart was hungry for love, but my discernment was still developing. In that season, the Lord, in His mercy, sent a prophet to speak directly into my life. With the brightest smile on her face, she told me that God had a man for me, a husband. He said this man would be a little older than me, that he would love my spunk, and that he would provide me the freedom to choose whether I wanted to work or not, because God knew that I worried about finances.

That word came at the very beginning of my salvation, before I had proven anything, before I had matured spiritually, and before I understood what walking with God truly required. From that moment forward, I carried a promise. And for the next ten years, I waited.

There were moments of impatience, of course. Seasons where silence felt heavy and nothing seemed to be moving at all. But something remarkable happened in that waiting: I learned how to anchor myself to the promise instead of chasing the manifestation. Every man I dated during that season was measured, not against my emotions, but against the word God had spoken over my life. When they did not align, I moved on without anxiety, without panic, and without fear that I was missing my moment.

I did not need to manufacture an outcome. I did not need to force timing. I trusted that if God had spoken it, He was faithful to perform it. Waiting taught me discernment without desperation. It taught me how to desire something deeply without idolizing it. It taught me how to release relationships quickly when they were out of alignment, not because I was guarded, but because I was grounded. Even when I did not perceive God moving on my behalf concerning marriage, I never doubted that He was moving within me. And that made all the difference.

God is not a liar. If He has spoken a promise over your life, He is not waiting for you to force it into existence. He is waiting for you to trust Him enough to let Him bring it forth in His time. Faith is not proven by how fast something happens, but by how steadily we remain aligned while it doesn't.

The waiting season is not passive, it is deeply active. Prayer deepens. Sensitivity sharpens. Obedience becomes refined. What appears slow on the outside is often rapid transformation within. God does not waste waiting. He uses it to ensure that when the promise arrives, it does not become a burden, an idol, or a breaking point.

The assignment of this season is to remain submitted without stagnation and faithful without forcing. You are called to resist the urge to manipulate timing, manufacture movement, or compare your progress to others. This is the season to deepen prayer, sharpen discernment, and anchor your identity in God rather than outcomes. Waiting requires obedience without confirmation and trust without visible reinforcement. Your responsibility is not to accelerate the promise, but to remain aligned while God completes the work He began.

Possible Harvests:

- Renewed strength and emotional stability
- Discernment and spiritual sensitivity
- Deepened trust in God's character and timing
- Endurance that produces maturity and completeness
- Confidence rooted in obedience rather than outcomes

The Obedience Without Explanation Season

"Go from your country... to the land I will show you."
— **Genesis 12:1**

As a child, I was *very* inquisitive. If my mother asked me to thaw the chicken out in the sink and not the fridge, I asked "why?" If my father told me it was unacceptable to eat ice cream for dinner, I asked "why?" In fact, I questioned my parents, family, and teachers so much, that sometimes they irritably ran out of answers to give me. I often never understood their agitation with me after 30 minutes of continuous "why's," but as I matured in age, I understood, ironically, *why*. Sometimes, it's simply better to trust in the wisdom of the one giving the instruction, because they know the end goal they're trying to get you to achieve.

Likewise, God does not always explain Himself before He asks for obedience. Not as an act of cruelty, but as an act of intimacy. The problem for many believers, though, is the expectation that He *will*, or that He *must*, before a single step is taken. People begin to hide their disobedience behind the guise of "I'm waiting on clarity," or "I'm praying and waiting on God to reveal more." But, what if that isn't the way God wants to handle that particular season? Sometimes, He speaks in simple instructions, not detailed plans, inviting us to trust His voice more than our limited understanding. These are the seasons when faith is no longer theoretical, but lived, when obedience becomes the language of devotion. Obedience is not always born from understanding. Oftentimes, it's born from trust, and this season will truly expose whether or not you do.

In 2023, God led me into one of those sacred, stretching seasons, where surrender mattered more than certainty and trust mattered more than clarity. He asked me to do something that didn't make sense: Shut my business down and move my daughter and myself across the country from Maryland to California. There was no explanation, no timeline, no financial plan - just an instruction: Go.

At the time, it felt like punishment. I had built a level of stability that gave me comfort. I had a brick and mortar business, a rhythm, and a sense of security. But, God was not asking for my comfort. He was asking for my obedience. So I closed the doors and packed our lives into just four suitcases, selling anything I couldn't carry with me on the plane. I used the last of my money to book two one-way flights, and fixed my mind on the instruction God gave. There was no job waiting for me, no income promised, no savings to live off of, and no safety net beneath us. Only faith; faith that trusted God with the entirety of my life. Faith that didn't have to make sense. Faith that was willing to risk everything I had built with my own hands to freefall into the hands and will of God.

I was certain of the fact that I was moving across country. God continued to confirm the destination without explaining the journey. The name of my soon-to-be new city started to appear everywhere; on the side of moving trucks, on apartment buildings, on school signs, and even on license plates. I wasn't searching for it, but it kept finding me and reminding me that I heard correctly. Yet and still, God wasn't giving me details: He was giving me reassurance.

As the departure date grew closer, provision began to follow my obedience. It wasn't just the intent to move it was every step I took towards moving - steps that made the move *real*. People I knew reached out to me, sowing financial seeds that they had never given me before. People I didn't know even called to give, and gave. Some offered encouragement, some sent money, and the amounts made no logical sense for where I was in life. I didn't ask for any of it. But, I knew God had instructed it. By the time my daughter and I boarded that plane, three months of rent was already paid. Again, not because I had planned it, but because God had provided it through all of the people He used to give into my life as I moved forward in faith.

Obedience without explanation doesn't feel beautiful while you're living it. It feels heavy. It feels quiet. And, above all, it feels lonely. There were nights I stared at the ceiling wondering if I had misunderstood God. Days when fear tried to convince me that my faith was foolish. Moments when I wanted clarity more than courage. But clarity was never the assignment, trust was. I had to sit in this season to learn that God wasn't withholding information to frustrate or confuse me. He was withholding it to deepen me. When you move without understanding, you learn how to walk with God. When you leave without answers, you learn how to listen, and when you surrender without guarantees, you learn how to lean.

California didn't just change my address; It completely changed my posture. I learned how to build with heaven instead of hustle, how to create from conviction instead of comfort, and how to trust God in motion, not just in prayer. I had no idea of all the wonderful things God had in store for me. From that season of obedience, the Raven Makenzie brand was born, my candle company, GodScent, was revamped, my non-profit organization and ministry were given new strategy and grew internationally, and I met my husband. Not from strategy. Not from striving, but from surrender. What people see now is the fruit of obedience. What they didn't see was the faith. It cost me the life I had, to usher me into the life I desired. Above all, it cost me my mediocre faith to lead me into the true depths of God's love.

Obedience without explanation will always cost you something. But it will also reveal something. It reveals who you trust. It reveals who you follow. It reveals whether your faith is conditional or consecrated. God does not always explain before He moves. Sometimes He moves so you can learn to trust Him without explanation, and that kind of trust builds something eternal. This season, learn to obey step by step without demanding full understanding. Trust the Lord with all your heart, and lean not on your own understanding. (Proverbs 3:5-6).

Potential Harvest

This season produces:

- Sharpened discernment
- Deep intimacy with God
- Confidence in His voice

PART III:

Identity, Silence, and Inner Reconstruction

When God dismantles false identities to establish true ones. *"Your life is hidden with Christ in God."*
—Colossians 3:3

Seasons of Identity Refinement

To understand this season, we must first understand identity itself. Identity is often defined in many ways, but at its core, it answers one essential question: What qualities or beliefs distinguish you? For the believer, the answer is simple, though not always easy to live out, our identity is found in Christ.

Scripture tells us, "Therefore, if anyone is in Christ, the new creation has come: the old has gone, the new is here!" (2 Corinthians 5:17). From the moment you said yes to Christ, you were made new. The labels the world assigned to you no longer hold authority. The old has not merely been set aside; it has passed away. And what is dead can no longer govern what is alive.

Before Christ, we identify with the world. After Christ, we are called to identify with Him. Christ becomes the standard by which truth is measured in our lives. This raises an important question, not just who are you, but who do people say you are?

Jesus posed this same question to His disciples. "Who do people say that the Son of Man is?" They answered with a list of labels; John the Baptist, Elijah, Jeremiah, a prophet. Then Jesus turned the question inward: "But who do you say that I am?" Peter's response revealed something profound: truth about identity does not come from public opinion, but from the Father (Matthew 16:13–17).

Man misidentified Jesus, just as man often misidentifies us. Had Jesus accepted the labels people gave Him, He would have forfeited His purpose. Instead, He rested in what the Father had declared. This is the heart of identity refinement; learning to reject external labels and internal lies in favor of divine truth.

Identity refinement does not always announce itself loudly. It often disguises itself as confusion, insecurity, comparison, or misplaced desire. Outside of Christ, what we believe about ourselves is not truth, it is perception. And perception, when disconnected from God, leads to distortion.

Lost or misaligned identity can manifest in many ways: low self-worth, sexual confusion, addiction, striving, people-pleasing, or the need for validation. At the root of each is the same issue; identity being sourced from something other than God. This is why identity matters so deeply. Confidence, assurance, and self-worth are not self-generated; they are rooted in faith, faith in who God says He is and who He says we are.

"For it is God who works in you to will and to act in order to fulfill His good purpose" — **Philippians 2:13**.

When the world says you are nothing, God says you are chosen. When the world says you are defeated, God says you are more than a conqueror. When the world says you are rejected, God says you are beloved (Romans 8:37; 1 Peter 2:9; Jeremiah 31:3).

God designed identity to be unchanging, just as He is unchanging. Who He created you to be from the beginning is who He intended you to walk as until the end. Sin did not erase identity, it distorted our ability to see and accept it. Identity is not taken from us; it is either embraced or rejected. When we reject God's truth, we allow experiences, opinions, trauma, status, money, or performance to define us. Insecurities grow. Doubt settles in. Confidence erodes. But Christ has conquered this as well.

One truth captures this season perfectly: In the Kingdom, knowing Him is knowing yourself. Our truest identity is discovered through relationship. Christ is woven into the very fabric of who we are. Without fellowship with Him, we will always struggle to walk confidently in our destiny.

Seasons of identity refinement come to test what voice we believe. But when identity is restored in Christ, destiny becomes clear. The harvest of this season is not something external, it is you. The authentic you. The refined you. The you God always intended.

The assignment of this season is to reject false labels and fully submit to God's truth. You are called to examine where your identity has been shaped by experiences rather than Scripture, by wounds rather than wisdom, or by culture rather than Christ. This season requires intentional intimacy with God, through prayer, the Word, and honest self-reflection, so that His voice becomes louder than every competing narrative. Identity refinement is not about becoming someone new; it is about returning to who God already declared you to be. Your responsibility is to agree with heaven, even when it contradicts what you feel, remember, or have been told.

Possible Harvests:

- Spiritual confidence rooted in Christ, not performance
- Freedom from false labels and past definitions
- Clarity of purpose and calling

- Emotional stability and self-worth grounded in truth
- Boldness to walk authentically and unapologetically

The Calling Season

"Before I formed you in the womb I knew you; before you were born I set you apart." — **Jeremiah 1:5**

In 2015, only a few brief months after I had surrendered my life to Christ, I entered into a season of fasting and praying that brought with it revelation of what God desired from my life. I had a deep knowing of two things for certain: First, God wanted to use me. Second, He would use me beyond my wildest dreams.

I saw visions of platforms, ministering the gospel and ushering in waves of revival. I saw properties I would own, early learning centers, businesses, farms and land, all the to the glory of God and the advancement of His gospel. I knew night after night, dream after dream, that the Lord was confirming His will in me. It left me with a burning desire to move speedily ino the what I saw, moving without wisdom, without structure, without the clarity of "how" or "when," and called it "living by faith." In reality, I was moving ignorantly with minimal success, carried by te grace of

God. Like many of you reading this, I misunderstood one key fact about the calling season: The calling came as a gift; it didn't require me to move, it required me to receive.

The calling season is marked by revelation without release. God speaks to who you are long before He assigns what you will do. This is why calling often awakens desire without providing direction; it reveals identity before timing. Much of the time, we discern accurately that we have been called by God, and make the mistake of rushing its fulfillment - this is where we lose the plot. Moreover, this is where the enemy plays his hand to get believers to fall into the confusion of "Did God *really* said that?"

Scripture reminds us that calling precedes action:

"Before I formed you in the womb I knew you; before you were born I set you apart." — **Jeremiah 1:5**

Calling is not urgency. It is recognition. Its revelation does not demand you to move now, it requires you to sit and seek - timing, process, and alignment. In this season, God establishes belonging before responsibility. He names you before He sends you. This can feel uncomfortable because clarity arrives *without* permission to move. Yet, this restraint is intentional. Vision without restraint produces pride, but vision carried with humility produces endurance. Thus, the calling season is an invitation to listen, not rush.

Throughout Scripture, God reveals purpose long before He releases permission to act, and how a person responds to that revelation matters just as much as the revelation itself. Consider David. When Samuel anointed David as king, David was still a boy tending sheep. The oil was real, the calling was legitimate, the promise was clear, but the throne was not immediate. David did not rush to demand position, confront Saul, or announce himself as king. Instead, he returned to the fields. He learned obedience in obscurity, faithfulness in small assignments, and restraint under pressure. David was named before he was sent, and because he honored the process, his calling matured into authority rather than pride (1 Samuel 16).

Did you return to your field when the Lord called you, or did you drop everything you were doing to run to the next thing? Stewardship is our ultimate responsibility. God does not tell us to forsake what He previously entrusted to us to steward, to rush into the beginnings of a new season. In fact, quite the opposite is true. It's when He finds us faithful in the mundane, the simple, the small, that He entrusts us with the stewardship of a new thing, a bigger thing.

Now consider Joseph. Joseph was also given a vision; clear, symbolic, and prophetic. God showed him who he would become and how others would one day bow. But Joseph spoke what he saw without discernment for timing or audience. What was meant to be nurtured in secrecy was announced prematurely. The result was not immediate fulfillment, but betrayal, isolation, and imprisonment. Joseph's calling was not revoked, but his process became longer and more painful because revelation was released without restraint (Genesis 37). Both David and Joseph were called. Both were shown purpose. But only one paired revelation with wisdom at the beginning. This is the tension of the calling season.

As I mentioned earlier, God will establish belonging before responsibility in the calling season. Your desire to fulfill that calling is awakened but direction necessary to carry out that calling is withheld. The calling season is not a demand to act. The will of God is not fragile, and His purposes do not prevail on your shoulders alone. Do not allow the enemy to make you feel rushed, as if moving in step with God now will cost you the promise of purpose later. Haste invites mistakes, and when we rush ahead of God, we discover that guidance is lost when the One who leads is left trailing behind.

Here, God teaches you how to hold what He has shown you without rushing ahead of Him. You'll learn how to possess calling without rushing its fulfillment – a trait you'll need to carry in ministry, marriage, the work force, and elsewhere. He invites you to sit with the vision, seek His timing, submit to His process, and align your heart before your hands ever move. Those who honor this season discover that waiting does not weaken the calling. Rather, it strengthens it. Your assignment is to receive without striving. You are not required to announce, defend, or pursue what God has revealed. You are required to hold it with reverence and patience. As Romans 8:30 reminds us, calling is part of a divine order, one that God Himself completes. Those who honor calling without acceleration are prepared for obedience without collapse.

Potential Harvest

When stewarded well, the calling season produces:

- Identity clarity rooted in God
- Direction without pressure
- Desire purified of ambition

The Concealment Season

"For you died, and your life is hidden with Christ in God." — **Colossians 3:3**

The concealment season is one of God's greatest mercies, though it is rarely recognized as such while we are in it. More often, it is misinterpreted as neglect or delay. This season often feels like obscurity, silence, or being overlooked. You may know what God has spoken, yet nothing or no one externally confirms it. You feel the weight of life and purpose without validation, but fully understand what God has called you into. The key to understanding seasons of concealment is this: Concealment is not God withholding *from* us; it is God withholding *us* for a time. What God conceals, He protects. What He hides, He preserves. What He covers, He keeps. Concealment is not inactivity or neglect; it is formation without the dangers of premature exposure.

Scripture does not say our lives are *lost* in God, but *hidden*. Hidden implies intention. Hidden implies care.

Hidden implies timing. God conceals before He reveals. He covers before He commissions. He forms before He displays. To be hidden by God is not to be forgotten; it is to be guarded.

In a culture that celebrates visibility and immediate fruit, we often misread the great mercy of concealment as punishment. We typically tend to equate progress with movement, and faithfulness with being seen. However, God measures seasons differently. Some of His deepest work happens in silence. Some of His greatest preparation occurs in obscurity. We must learn to understand that visibility without maturity is not favor; it is vulnerability. God often hides His servants not because they are unready to *do*, but because they are unready to *be seen*.

In 2017, about three years after I began walking with Christ, I entered what I now recognize as a prolonged season of "doing." At the time, it felt like obedience. I was responding to everything God had shown me. What I did not yet understand was that calling is not activated by activity, it is stewarded through stillness and intimacy. I had little regard for stillness, listening, and direction before the Lord. I also lacked discernment for the areas of my life where God was actively concealing me.

Full of zeal, I ran ahead of God. I taught Bible studies, hosted ministry gatherings in my home, built businesses, prophesied to crowds, wrote two books, recorded podcasts, and more. From the outside, it looked productive. But when the years passed, I was left with a sobering truth: I had accomplishments, but little fruit behind them. I began to ask questions I was afraid to voice.

Why, after all I had done, was there so little support? Why did it feel like no one truly saw what I was building? Why did nothing seem to last?

The ache of invisibility followed me into my personal life. Even in relationships, I felt hidden. The truest parts of my character seemed shielded from view. I was misjudged, misunderstood, and misnamed, treated in ways that contradicted who I knew myself to be. It was humiliating. Breakup after breakup. Argument after argument. Trying to convince the men I dated that I was somebody, that I had substance, that I mattered. My desire to be understood turned into striving. My longing to be loved became pushing - pushing to be seen, pushing to be valued. And still, nothing changed.

Eventually, exhaustion gave way to surrender. I stopped asking *why* and asked *how long*. "How much longer, Lord, until I'm seen? How much longer until I'm valued and understood?" The Lord answered me simply: "You are hidden by My hand. Not as punishment, but as protection." This simple revelation reframed everything for me.

No longer did I care that I was hidden - I understood at this point that it was inevitable. I realized I was not being hidden *from* people, but I was being hidden *by* God, for my ultimate good, and His sovereign plan for my life. And as it turned out, I gained clarity of an unknown truth: There are rules to being hidden.

The first rule: God hides to protect something. When God hides something or someone, the purpose is never to bring shame. He conceals what is precious, vulnerable, valuable, or unfinished as a means of preservation. Our greatest example of this is found in Genesis 3 after the fall of man, where God places two Cherubim at the entrance of the Garden of Eden to "guard the path." (Genesis 3:24). Not simply as a means to punish Adam and Eve for sinning, but to protect holy ground, and the place where God first had pure, unhindered, beautiful communion and connection with mankind. This act of concealment not only displayed the effects of sin and God's response in the earth, it displayed the heart of God in His intent to preserve something good from being tainted.

The second rule: God develops in private what He will display in purpose. In concealment, roots are afforded an opportunity to go deeper, strength increases, and identity is formed without pressure. If you've read my second book, *Wisdom from Eden,* you likely already have a sound understanding of this concept from the chapter titled "No Root,

No Fruit." I won't go too deep on the subject here, but want to emphasize one core truth about this rule: Hidden does not mean stagnant. Consider a fruit tree. Its root system must be fully developed, strong, and vast in order for the trunk, branches, leaves, and subsequent fruit to grow abundantly. It's the roots that feed the fruit! No roots, no fruit. What God develops underground in your life earns you the fruit, the oil, and the permission, to be on full display in purpose when the time is right. Your fruit is birthed after the roots, not before.

The third rule: Concealment is preparation for proximity. God will often conceal to deepen intimacy and eliminate distance and distractions. Oftentimes, before God reveals something to the world, He draws it closer to Himself. In the book of Exodus, God conceals Moses not to remove him, but to bring him closer to His glory without destroying him. (Exodus 33:21-22). In this case, concealment was not absence, but both protection and intimacy that fueled Moses' leadership. It allowed for a certain closeness to God - a level of anointing that others simply couldn't carry or access, which aided Moses' ministry towards the people of Israel.

The fourth rule: God covers what is not yet built for public weight. Exposure requires capacity - capacity that, as we discussed earlier, must be developed in confidence. What God conceals is graciously spared from premature demand, criticism, and spiritual warfare. Consider King David who was anointed in private as a boy before being revealed as king. (1 Samuel 16:11-13). Had he not had the privacy of being a shepherd boy learning to tend to the sheep of his own field, it is likely that he would have lacked the wisdom and grace necessary to shepherd Israel. The public weight of kingship may have likely crushed him, as the demands and cries of the people proved to be overwhelming. Thankfully, his role privately had an opportunity to mature through the grace of concealment, and when he was revealed publicly, God was able to utilize David's strengths in battle, as well as for leadership, all to His glory.

The fifth rule: Not all concealment is secrecy. God's hiding is holy, not deceptive. Though He withholds access to some things, He never withholds truth. The book of Proverbs reminds us that it is the glory of God to conceal a matter. (Proverbs 25:2). Thus, we understand that concealment sometimes serves as a boundary in the hands of God.

The sixth rule: Concealment carries divine intention. Every hidden season you encounter carries a purpose, and nothing God covers is wasted. The book of Ecclesiastes reminds us that to everything there is a season under sun. And yes, this includes concealment too. When you find yourself hidden by the hand of God, anchor yourself to the reality that there is a reason God is concealing you, even if you can't perceive it.

The seventh rule: Revelation is always timed. This ties in heavily with the sixth rule, given there is a time for concealment, and a time for revelation. God reveals - you, your assignment, your business, your ministry, your husband or wife, etc. - when readiness meets assignment. Galatians 4:4 reminds us that "When the fullness of time had come, God sent His Son." It is only after the fullness of time regarding your preparation that the Lord launch you into the purpose(s) He readied you for.

The eighth and final rule: What God hides reveals what He values. God has no interest in concealing what is disposable; He conceals what is destined. The things heaven chooses to guard are never random or carelessly chosen. Protection is always an expression of priority. John 17:12 references Jesus saying "I have kept them safe...not one has been lost." He protected the disciples because they were essential; they carried the message, mission, and movement of the Kingdom. Their preservation was directly connected to their purpose. In the same way, what God conceals in your life is often what carries the greatest responsibility to the Kingdom. The more weight something holds in the future, the more carefully it is handled in the present, because more frequently the enemy will try to attack it. Hidden things are not forgotten things; they are guarded things. God conceals what carries destiny.

It took the revelation of these rules for me to realize I was not concealed because I lacked value, but because I carried it. I was not delayed, but simply guarded. I realized I had been striving against mercy. God's concealment protects us from building without foundation, from being applauded before being anchored, from mistaking affirmation for identity. What gets revealed too early, the world will demand you sustain. What God conceals, He Himself sustains.

Concealment precedes commissioning. Joseph is hidden in a pit and a prison before he governs a nation. Moses is hidden in Midian before he confronts Pharaoh. David is hidden among sheep before he ascends the throne. Even Jesus is hidden for thirty years before three years of public ministry. This concealment may have appeared as absence, but ultimately it was preparation for each person to successfully carry what the Lord has commissioned them to carry.

The concealment season teaches us to obey without applause and to trust without recognition. When your life is hidden with Christ in God, you are not responsible for visibility, He is. Your responsibility is formation, faithfulness, and obedience in secret. When God decides to reveal what He has concealed, no striving will be required.

What is revealed by God will be sustained by God. Until then, concealment is a season to steward, because what God hides today, He will unveil in His time. When He does, it will carry the weight of His hand, not the weakness of our striving.

If the season you're in feels like obscurity, silence, or being overlooked, partnered with unshakable belief in what God has spoken regarding your life, yet nothing externally confirms it, you may be in a concealment season. Your assignment is to remain submitted without striving. Resist the urge to self-introduce what God has not yet released. Those who are hidden well are not undone when visibility comes.

Potential Harvest

When honored, concealment produces:
- Security in identity
- Freedom from performance
- Protection from premature warfare
- Humility that sustains authority

The Testing Season / Seasons of Silence

"My people are destroyed for lack of knowledge."
— Hosea 4:6 (NIV)

We have all been here before, fully surrendered to God, burning with passion for His will, eager to walk in His way. And then, suddenly, we find ourselves in silence. We no longer hear Him clearly. We struggle to recognize His movement or understand what He is doing. Confusion sets in, frustration follows, until we remember a principle most of us learned long before adulthood: the teacher is always silent during the test.

Testing is not punishment, it is proof. God allows testing not to condemn us, but to confirm what preparation has already produced. Scripture tells us plainly, "The Lord your God led you... to test you, to know what was in your heart" (Deuteronomy 8:2). Testing reveals what is already there. The pressure does not create character; it exposes it.

A mentor once repeated this principle to me often. At the time, I understood it intellectually, but not spiritually. Years later, reflecting on the many tests I took from grade school through college, I realized how consistently true it was. During every defining exam, the teacher was silent, not absent, not disengaged, but attentive to how I problem solved; attentive to how I responded. The silence was intentional, because the moment required demonstration rather than instruction.

Tests never come without preparation. While quizzes may arrive unexpectedly and serve to keep us alert during the learning process, tests carry weight. They assess readiness. They determine whether the material has been absorbed deeply enough to advance. How much more does our Father in heaven operate with intention? God allows quizzes; small trials, disruptions, and challenges to keep our attention focused on Him. In His grace, these moments are open book. We can ask Him questions. We can seek wisdom. We can pray, fast, and lean on His Word. These experiences are rehearsals, foreshadows of what will later be required of us. But when the test comes, heaven grows quiet. But, you must know this: The silence is not abandonment, it is confirmation.

Testing seasons are designed to reveal integrity, not to induce fear. They expose whether we will apply what we have learned without reassurance or immediate relief. Will we freeze and wait to be rescued, or will we stand and use the tools God has already placed within us? Will we pray? Will we fast? Will we respond with wisdom instead of panic? Have we studied to show ourselves approved, or will we falter for lack of knowledge?

> *"Study and do your best to present yourself to God approved, a workman [tested by trial] who has no reason to be ashamed, accurately handling the word of truth."* — **2 Timothy 2:15 (AMP)**

I experienced the testing season most recently, when my very new marriage was put to the test. My husband and I began arguing over the simplest things, and the only instinct I knew was to run. Before marriage, the moment fear surfaced or trust wavered, I would end the relationship. I would cut the person off entirely, treating them as disposable, because of pain and trauma I carried for years.

But in my single season, God taught me something different. He taught me to stop running and to engage the present moment with clarity and discernment. So when those same emotions resurfaced in my marriage, the urge to flee, to disengage, to protect myself, I was faced with a choice. I could react from who I used to be, or I could apply what God had already taught me.

In those moments, it was this very book that reminded me: if you abandon the process, you abandon the harvest. There was nothing happening in front of me that God had not already prepared me for. I was equipped to engage the moment, to apply wisdom, and to bring resolution rather than retreat. So instead of running from my husband, I stayed. I listened. I applied discernment. I drew from the vault of wisdom God had already deposited in me.

These moments arise often, not because God is cruel, but because He fortifies what He has taught us through testing. What we do not practice, we lose. Just like muscles that weaken when they are unused, wisdom must be exercised to remain strong. Testing does not mean God is displeased. Silence does not mean He is absent. It means He is asking you to draw from what is already within you. Testing seasons are not about learning something new, they are about proving what has already been learned.

God desires to use us, but He also desires that we want to be used enough to remain obedient under pressure. Advancement has always required testing. We did not graduate academically without exams, and we will not advance spiritually without demonstrating faithfulness when obedience is costly.

Do not confuse God's silence with His absence. Just as teachers quietly walk the room during an exam - observing, monitoring, and noting progress - so does God. Silence does not mean He has stepped away; it means the moment requires demonstration rather than direction.

Scripture gives us one of the clearest examples of this in Abraham's test with Isaac. God had already spoken the promise. Isaac was the evidence that God was faithful. Yet before Abraham was sent forward into the fullness of his assignment, his obedience was tested. God asked him to place the promise back on the altar, not because He intended to take it, but because He needed to reveal what truly ruled Abraham's heart. Heaven was silent as Abraham climbed the mountain, but God was watching. And at the moment obedience was proven, provision appeared.

The test did not negate the promise, it confirmed Abraham was ready to carry it. In the same way, God allows testing to complete what preparation has begun. James reminds us, "The testing of your faith produces perseverance. Let perseverance finish its work so that you may be mature and complete, lacking nothing" (James 1:3–4). Testing does not interrupt the process; it perfects it. What is proven under pressure is what can be trusted with promotion, and if we falter, God does not discard us. He allows us to walk the test again, not as punishment, but as preparation, until obedience becomes instinct and faith is no longer conditional on clarity.

The assignment of this season is clear: remain obedient under pressure, without guarantee or immediate relief. Testing seasons, often experienced as seasons of silence, are not designed to frustrate us. They are designed with harvest in mind. They confirm readiness, fortify faithfulness, and reveal whether our trust is anchored in God's voice, or in His character alone. Silence does not mean God has left. It means the test is revealing what preparation has produced, and there is always a harvest on the other side.

Potential Harvest

Testing produces:

- Proven faith
- Spiritual credibility
- Confidence rooted in God

PART IV:

Strength Under Pressure

Learning endurance, faith, and trust under sustained weight. *"Tribulation produces perseverance; perseverance, character"* — **Romans 5:3-4**

Seasons of Lost Hope

Many people mistake the loss of hope for the loss of faith, but the two are not the same. Faith declares that God is able. Hope holds the expectation that He will act. When hope begins to erode, faith is often left to carry the weight alone. And while faith can endure, it was never designed to journey without hope. Scripture consistently binds the two together, because hope is the posture that keeps faith forward-facing.

Becoming a believer does not exempt us from seasons where hope feels fragile. It does not shield us from disappointment, fatigue, or the quiet discouragement that accumulates over time. I am not someone who will suggest that following Christ means you will never lose hope. I have been there more times than I can count. There have been seasons where defeat felt close, where the struggle seemed endless, where healing felt delayed, and where financial pressure refused to lift. These experiences are not evidence of weak faith; they are part of the human condition.

Sometimes we grow tired. Sometimes we become emotionally exhausted. Sometimes doubt does not arrive loudly, but slowly, subtly reshaping how we interpret our circumstances and the promises we once held with confidence. Seasons of lost hope are not failures of belief; they are moments of weariness that reveal how deeply we need God to restore not just our faith, but our expectation of His goodness.

Seasons of lost hope often follow prolonged waiting, repeated disappointment, or labor that appears to yield no visible return. They do not arrive loudly; they arrive subtly, through silence, delay, and unmet expectations. Hope rarely disappears all at once. It fades slowly, worn down by time and discouragement. Scripture makes room for this reality, though. The Bible does not pretend that God's people never lose hope. In fact, it shows us what God does when they do.

"Hope deferred makes the heart sick, but a longing fulfilled is a tree of life." — **Proverbs 13:12**

Hope deferred does not make the heart sinful. It makes it weary. And God is not offended by weary hearts.

I remember when the Lord spoke to me and said, *"My people believe that I can do it. They simply struggle to believe that I will do it for them."* That sentence exposed a pattern

I had observed not only in my own life, but in the lives of many believers, often my own brothers and sisters in faith. We believe in God's power in theory, yet wrestle with believing in His personal intention. We trust that He moves, but quietly question whether He will move on our behalf.

I have shared throughout this book that I waited ten years for my husband. What I had not shared until now is that during that waiting, there came moments when hope began to erode. Disappointment followed disappointment. Promise after promise was tested against reality, and somewhere along the way, something shifted within me. I never stopped believing God *could* do it. I simply stopped believing He *would*, at least not for me.

The same pattern emerged in ministry. I was certain of what God had spoken and confident that the calling was real. I continued to labor, to serve, to build, and to pour. Yet as time passed without visible movement, confirmation, or fruit, my posture began to change. I remained obedient, but my expectation quietly disengaged. I did not abandon the work, but I did abandon hope.

This is the subtle danger of prolonged seasons of waiting and testing: not disobedience, but quiet resignation, or lost hope. It is the slow acceptance of the idea that obedience is required, but expectation is optional, that our labor must continue, even if the promise never arrives.

When hope is surrendered, faith becomes mechanical, and perseverance turns into survival. This is where many believers find themselves, faithful in action, yet internally convinced that their labor may ultimately be in vain.

Thankfully, you're not alone. Scripture gives us many examples of faithful people who wrestled with hope. John the Baptist believed Jesus was the Messiah. He was sent to prepare the way. Yet while imprisoned, isolated, and tormented by oppressive thoughts, he sent word to Jesus asking, "Are you the one who is to come, or should we look for another?" (Matthew 11:3). Even in his doubt, Jesus responded with assurance and honor.

Peter boldly confessed that Jesus was the Son of the living God, yet denied Him three times when fear crept in. Jesus knew Peter's faith would fail for a moment, but He also knew it would return. And when it did, Peter was restored and commissioned to strengthen others. Elijah called down fire from heaven on Mount Carmel, yet fled in fear when Jezebel threatened his life. In his despair, Elijah asked God to take his life. God did not rebuke him. He fed him. He let him rest. He strengthened him for the journey ahead and reassigned him with purpose (1 Kings 19). The pattern is consistent: even when hope falters, God responds with compassion. Lost hope does not mean the promise has expired. It means the soul has grown tired of disappointment. This is why this season is dangerous. Not because God withdraws, but because *we* might. When hope fades, people stop preparing. They stop watching, and they stop positioning themselves for what God said would come. Not out of unbelief, but out of self-protection.

Scripture reminds us, *"Now faith is the substance of things hoped for..."* (Hebrews 11:1). Faith draws its substance from hope. When hope is weakened, belief begins to falter, not because faith has disappeared, but because its foundation has been shaken. If the enemy can attack where we hope, he can undermine how we believe. And when what we believe God for becomes distorted, what we can receive is often affected. Jesus speaks directly to this connection when He says, *"You can pray for anything, and if you have faith, you will receive it"* (Matthew 21:22). Yet, God does not shame us in seasons where hope has been depleted. He does not withdraw or rebuke; He restores. Rather than anchoring hope to outcomes, He re-centers it in Himself. *"May the God of hope fill you with all joy and peace as you trust in Him..."* (Romans 15:13). Before promises are fulfilled externally, hope is often rebuilt internally. For this reason, seasons of lost hope are not evidence of abandonment; they are invitations into deeper trust, where expectation is no longer rooted in circumstances, but in the unchanging character of God.

In this season, the assignment is not to perform hope when you are weary of waiting. Too many believers feel pressure to smile through pain, to appear strong when their inner world is unraveling. But God has never required pretense. He does not ask us to mask our reality or deny our grief. Forced optimism is not faith, and pretending does not produce healing.

The assignment of this season is surrender, not resignation, but honest release. It is learning how to place what you no longer have the strength to carry back into God's hands, while allowing hope to remain alive without demanding immediate outcomes. Hope in this season is not loud or emotional; it is quiet trust that rests in who God is, even when what He has promised feels distant. This is the work of lost-hope seasons: not striving to feel better, but choosing to stay anchored.

First, stick to what God told you. His Word is objective truth. Remind yourself of what He has already done, recall His faithfulness, and return to His promises. Second, rebuke the devourer. The enemy comes to steal, kill, and destroy. Do not allow his whispers to lead you into despair and take you from bad to worse. God's sheep know His voice. Reject every thought that contradicts God's truth. Third, ask for help. Do not isolate yourself. Sometimes strength comes through the prayers of others. You are part of the body of Christ, and no part is meant to suffer alone. Our hope may be fragile, but it is indeed hard to kill. Choose hope the same way you choose life. The harvest is on the other side of perseverance. And when you endure this season, you will find that what you harvest is greater faith, deeper trust, and hope that no longer collapses under pressure.

Possible Harvest:

- Renewed expectation
- Faith strengthened
- Discernment
- Endurance
- Steady Hope

Seasons of Learning Faith

Faith is, without a doubt, the central ingredient to walking the Christ-like life. Without it, we cannot please God (Hebrews 11:6). As with many things in a believer's walk, faith is not passive, accidental, or inherited; it is a choice an individual must make. Consider this: Long before you learned how to trust God deeply, you had to exercise faith just to come to Him. You believed that He is who He says He is. You believed that His Word is true. Even now, you heard Him speak and believe in more for your life; otherwise, you would not even be reading this book.

Every prayer you pray, every act of obedience, every moment of worship, every step of service, and every act of love requires faith. And yet, faith remains one of the most misunderstood concepts within the Christian walk. Many believers claim to have faith, but struggle to live by it fully. It requires a level of sacrifice and discomfort that many find too difficult to bear. This is why seasons of learning faith exist; not to introduce faith, but to mature it. So, what is faith? In summary, it can be distilled into two essential elements: confidence and assurance.

> *"Now faith is confidence in what we hope for and assurance about what we do not see."* — **Hebrews 11:1 (NIV)**

Confidence, simply put, is firm trust. Assurance is settled certainty, and together, they form a working definition of faith: a firm trust in God and confident assurance in what He has promised, even when it is not yet visible.

I like to visualize faith as a guardrail. Imagine a dark and winding road, where all light has been extinguished. This is often what the faith walk can feel like: uncertainty, no clear sense of direction, waiting on the light to reveal the path and direction beneath your feet. But then comes the guardrail. It's positioned parallel to the road, guarding you from going off course. Even if you could not see, the guardrail serves as a boundary, a sure sign that the road does not lead in a certain direction. Though we may not see the road, we have a constant assurance that keeps us dedicated from drifting off the path. That is faith: The guardrail that anchors us in our walk with Christ, and allows us to believe beyond what our senses can confirm. It is the foundation of the Christian life.

What many fail to understand is that initial faith is not mature faith. Seasons of learning faith are where belief - no matter its level of maturity - is tested, exercised, stretched, and refined: Where faith is not static, but further undergoes development. Here, where you begin is rarely where you end.

God is both the originator and perfecter of faith, so we must be careful to allow Him due process to develop faith within us. Faith reached its fullness through Christ, and He now invites us to grow into that same maturity. No one is born into unwavering faith; it's a muscle that must be trained. This is not something you go to bed lacking and wake up full of the next day. Faith is formed through experience, obedience, and surrender. God intentionally allows situations that require us to trust Him more deeply, because faith cannot grow without use. For many, this is a great discomfort.

We move from faith to faith (Romans 1:17), not away from faith, but deeper into it. Much like standing at the shoreline of the ocean and looking out at the water, then slowly stepping away from the shore and into its depths. It is the same body of water, yet it is experienced differently. The deeper you go, the more trust is required, but also, the more you understand about the water that you never would have gained the knowledge of by standing on the shoreline alone. In the same way, God does not call us to abandon faith, but to enter it more fully, learning to trust Him beyond what feels safe or familiar. We will never outgrow or graduate from faith lessons. It is something we continually develop through each new dimension. Faith, like love, expands as we walk with God, and each season becomes an invitation to believe Him more fully than before.

In seasons of learning faith, you may encounter circumstances that challenge everything you thought you believed. Just remember in these moments that God moves us forward not to break us, but to build up greater trust. You must resist the temptation to confine God to familiar outcomes, remove Him from the box you've placed Him in, and believe not only that He *can*, but that He *will*. The assignment of this season is to practice trust before proof, as God invites you to move beyond verbal belief and into lived belief. You are called to align your actions with what you say you believe about God: His character, His promises, and His faithfulness. Your faith must shift from concept to daily conduct.

In this season, examine where you are hesitating, delaying, or waiting for confirmation before obedience. Faith grows when obedience comes first. This assignment requires you to act in alignment with God's Word even when outcomes are unclear, timelines feel stretched, or emotions resist agreement. You are not asked to manufacture results, but to respond to God as if His Word is already settled.

Additionally, you are invited to identify the areas where disappointment, fear, or comparison have weakened your confidence in God's willingness to move on your behalf. Faith matures when you choose to believe that what God has done for others, He is able and willing to do for you. This season asks you to replace passive hope with active expectation and to steward your faith through consistent obedience, prayer, preparation, and praise. Faith is not proven in ease; it is refined in uncertainty. Remain steady, obedient, and expectant, trusting that God is working even when you cannot yet see the fruit.

Possible Harvests of the Faith Season

- Trust
- Confidence in God
- Spiritual Maturity
- Peace
- Preparation for Greater Responsibility
- Endurance

PART V:

Restoration, Healing, and Deliverance

God restores what was strained, broken, or wounded.
"He restores my soul" — **Psalm 23:3**

Seasons of Rest

Seasons of rest are just as essential as any other season we live through, yet they are often the most undervalued. Many of us associate rest with laziness, weakness, or wasted time. But if rest were insignificant, God would not have sanctified it. He would not have modeled it, commanded it, or promised it. Rest is both a season and a harvest. It renews the mind, restores the body, and re-centers the soul. It allows us to begin again, not depleted, but aligned.

> "By the seventh day God had finished the work He had been doing; so on the seventh day He rested from all His work. Then God blessed the seventh day and made it holy." — **Genesis 2:2-3**

> "Come to Me, all who are weary and burdened, and I will give you rest." — **Matthew 11:28**

> "God made the Sabbath for people, not people for the Sabbath." — **Mark 2:27**

Scripture makes it clear that rest is not optional, it is intentional. While many verses speak of a day of rest, there are moments when God leads us into an entire season of rest. These seasons often follow prolonged striving, misalignment, or burnout, especially when we have been building without God as the foundation.

I first encountered this season in 2016. The Lord instructed me to leave my full-time job, but I resisted. I reasoned, negotiated, and delayed until the environment became so toxic that I was forced to resign. It was then that I realized something sobering: God was not my true master. I had made work my idol. I missed church. I missed milestones with my daughter. I was mentally, physically, and emotionally exhausted, stretched thin across every area of life, yet excelling in none.

For ten months, I had no income. Where my schedule had once been filled with work, I intentionally filled it with Jesus. I sought Him daily, sometimes for hours at a time. I turned an extra bedroom into a prayer room and spent countless hours on the floor in His presence. For the first time in my life, I experienced true peace. Eventually, though, anxiety crept in. "God, I can't even tithe. What can I give You?" His response shifted my understanding entirely: "Tithe your time."

Soon after, God gave me a vision for a daycare. Provision followed quickly. Supplies appeared. Children came. Income flowed. But somewhere along the way, my motive shifted. What began as ministry slowly became driven by money. God had told me to tithe my time, not monetize it. I was out of season, building something God had shown me, but without Him as the foundation.

The pressure returned, the peace disappeared, and serving became draining. The thing I once loved became a burden. Eventually, I broke down and cried out to God. His response was gentle but firm:

> *"My yoke is easy, and My burden is light. You are exhausted because you have built this your way, in your time. Tear it down, and rebuild with Me."*
> *"Come to Me... and you will find rest for your souls."*
> — **Matthew 11:28-30**

> *"My ways are higher than your ways."* — **Isaiah 55:8**

I closed my daycare on November 9, 2018. It was the second time I walked away from an income, and the second time I was surrounded by peace. God showed me that I had created my own burden by chasing provision instead of purpose. When I finally rested, He restored me. That season of rest became the foundation for everything that followed, including this book. But, this lesson did not remain in the past.

In 2025, I encountered another season that required rest, this time at a deeper level. I was newly engaged and planning a wedding, preparing for my bonus daughter to move into our home, building two ministries simultaneously, working two jobs, and attending school full time. On paper, everything looked productive. It even looked spiritual. I believed I was walking in the will of God because I was doing so much for God, but the fruit told a different story.

I was exhausted; mentally, emotionally, spiritually, and physically. I could not give anything one hundred percent because I was trying to give everything all at once. Burnout crept in quietly and then took over completely. I became emotionally unstable, overwhelmed, and reactive. The woman God had called me to be was buried beneath responsibility, expectation, and performance. The only option was to stop.

I had to put things down, good things, even God things, so that I could rest, refocus, and rebuild on the foundation of Christ. The hardest part was letting go. I had convinced myself that my doing was obedience, when in reality, my doing had become performance. I was no longer operating from overflow, I was operating from pressure. And pressure, no matter how noble it appears, is not peace.

God reminded me that His will is never sustained by burnout. His assignments do not require emotional collapse to be fulfilled. Rest was not a step backward; it was a return to alignment. In that season, God shifted my focus back to my family, back to intimacy with Him, and back to building from wholeness rather than hustle. Thus, the revised version of this book was born.

You can be doing the right things with the wrong foundation. And when that happens, rest becomes mercy. God will always interrupt performance to preserve purpose. Rest is not the abandonment of calling, it is the protection of it.

"Peace I leave with you; My peace I give you."
— John 14:27

"The peace of God... will guard your hearts and your minds in Christ Jesus." **— Philippians 4:6-7**

Seasons of rest are not wasted. They rebuild, realign, and restore. They teach us to pour from overflow, not emptiness. They remind us that we are not sustained by effort, but by God. Seasons of rest allow us to harvest peace.

The assignment of this season is to stop striving and start abiding. You are called to release control, dismantle what was built outside of God's rhythm, and trust Him enough to pause without panic. Rest requires humility, and the willingness to admit exhaustion, misalignment, or burnout. In this season, obedience looks like stillness, prayer, recalibration, and restraint. Your responsibility is not to produce, but to receive. What God restores in rest cannot be achieved through effort alone.

Possible Harvests:

- Peace
- Emotional, spiritual, and physical renewal
- Clarity of purpose and direction
- Freedom from burnout and performance
- Strength to rebuild with God as the foundation

Seasons of Deliverance

Seasons of deliverance are among the most misunderstood and yet one of the most necessary seasons believers will ever walk through. Deliverance is not rare, dramatic, or reserved for extreme cases. It is a repeating season that appears whenever God desires to remove what threatens our freedom, clarity, and intimacy with Him. While this chapter does not attempt to exhaustively teach every dimension of deliverance, it offers foundational understanding and spiritual clarity meant to stir discernment and invite deeper study. Deliverance and healing are closely connected, and because both are woven deeply into my own journey as a believer, they are handled here with reverence, balance, and truth.

In Short, deliverance is release from bondage, spiritual, emotional, mental, or physical. It is God's act of rescuing us from captivity and oppression, breaking chains that restrict His life within us. In Hebrew, the word most often associated with deliverance is *natsal*, which means to snatch away, rescue, tear free, plunder, or strip from the enemy. These are not passive words. Deliverance is decisive, authoritative, and forceful. It confronts bondage directly and removes it at the root. Deliverance addresses the source of oppression, while healing addresses the damage *left behind*. Healing flows from God's power; deliverance flows from His authority. Both are expressions of His mercy and love, but they function differently.

Jesus clarified this distinction when He said that He had given His followers authority to trample on snakes and scorpions and to overcome all the power of the enemy (Luke 10:19). In this passage, two different Greek words are used. The authority given to believers is *exousia*, which refers to regal authority, or the right to command. The enemy's power referenced here is *dunamis*, which refers to raw strength or influence. Satan still possesses influence, but he no longer holds authority. Authority belongs to Christ, and by extension, to those who are in Him. Deliverance operates from authority, not force, and healing restores the damage from what authority removes.

Authority is not a formula, a chant, or something borrowed or mimicked. It flows only from a relationship with Christ. Scripture gives us a sobering example when the sons of Sceva attempted to cast out demons by invoking the name of Jesus without knowing Him. The spirits responded, *"Jesus I know, and Paul I know about, but who are you?"* (Acts 19:15). The name of Jesus is not a spell. It carries weight only when spoken by those submitted to Him. Authority is granted, not assumed. Jesus gave authority to His disciples because they were with Him, and because all authority belongs to Christ in heaven and on earth, the enemy's influence is subordinate, not sovereign. The Spirit of Christ within us is greater than the spirit at work in the world. NOTE: This does not negate medical, psychological, or practical responsibility, but acknowledges that spiritual influence can coexist with natural causes.

Deliverance becomes necessary when demonic influence gains access to a person's life. This influence appears primarily in two ways: oppression and possession. Oppression is external pressure meant to influence behavior, emotions, or thought patterns, while possession is internal influence, where a demonic presence occupies territory within a person. Scripture affirms both realities. Jesus healed those whom the devil oppressed, and He cast demons out of those who were possessed. Deliverance is not sensational; it is biblical. Our battle is not with people, personalities, or circumstances, but with spiritual forces, principalities, powers, rulers of darkness, and spiritual wickedness in high places (Ephesians 6:12). As I've mentioned at the start of this book, what happens spiritually will eventually manifest naturally, whether in behavior, health, emotion, or thought.

Demonic influence requires access, and that access is granted through open doors, often unknowingly. These doors may include sexual immorality, substance abuse, occult practices, astrology, tarot, spirit guides, energy-based spiritual practices, necromancy, séances, or divination. When a door is opened, we do not get to choose what enters, only whether we seek freedom afterward. Not every struggle is caused by demonic activity, and we must be careful not to give Satan undue credit. However, neither should we ignore his strategies. Discernment is essential.

I would like to note here that deliverance is not the end of the process; it is the beginning of self-stewardship. God provides protection through the full armor described in Ephesians: truth, righteousness, peace, faith, salvation, and the Word. Just as we dress our physical bodies daily, we must dress our spirits daily. Neglect leaves us exposed. In addition to armor, God equips us with weapons: the Word of God, praise, the blood of Jesus, prayer and fasting, testimony, and the name of Jesus. Deliverance removes bondage, but discipline protects freedom.

The purpose of deliverance is not merely to remove oppression but to restore clarity, stability, and peace in your life. It returns authority to its rightful place and allows you, the believer, to walk upright, unencumbered, and whole. Deliverance is not shameful; it is merciful. It is God's response to His children when they are weary, entangled, or oppressed. And like every other season, deliverance has a harvest, one very much worth fighting for.

The assignment of the deliverance season is not fear, fixation, or obsession with the enemy; it is awareness, surrender, and obedience. This season invites you to allow God to expose what has quietly influenced you beneath the surface and to respond with humility rather than defensiveness. Deliverance requires honesty before God. It asks you to examine what doors may have been opened knowingly or unknowingly, what patterns have persisted despite prayer, and where peace has been consistently absent.

The work of this season is not self-diagnosis or condemnation, but submission: yielding areas of your life to the authority of Christ and trusting Him to remove what you cannot. This assignment also requires discipline. Deliverance must be stewarded. Freedom must be guarded. As God removes bondage, you are called to remain vigilant through prayer, the Word, worship, and daily dependence on Him. Deliverance is not a moment; it is a cooperation with God's authority that restores rightful order in your life.

In seasons of deliverance, allow God to exercise His authority to break chains, silence your oppressors, and remove what has influenced your life unlawfully. Deliverance is not the end of the work, but it is the beginning of restoration. Once the knife has been removed, the wound still needs care. Once the bondage is broken, the soul still needs repair. God not only frees His people; He heals them. Where deliverance deals with what held you captive, healing addresses what captivity left behind. And it is here, after release, that many believers discover the deeper work of God's power.

Possible Harvests:

- Freedom
- Restored peace of mind, emotional stability, and clarity
- Renewed authority and confidence in Christ
- Release from cycles of addiction, fear, torment, or confusion
- Strengthened spiritual discipline and sensitivity to God's voice
- Alignment

Seasons of Healing

In early 2025, I entered one of the most significant seasons of healing I have experienced to date. Those closest to me knew I was struggling within my marriage, in leadership, as a mother, and as an entrepreneur. As the weight of responsibility increased in each of these areas, so did my frustration, and I perceived as pressure from every direction slowly turned into anger and bitterness. I became difficult to be around without realizing it. The people I loved found themselves walking on eggshells, not because *they* had changed, but because I had not yet recognized what was rising within me. They could see that something in me was unsettled, but I couldn't.

I had been serving every area of my life from my own strength. In doing so, I unintentionally cultivated a space where resentment could grow. The issue, however, was not the demands of marriage, ministry, business, or motherhood. Those were not the source. They were merely the places where unresolved wounds surfaced. The anger I experienced did not originate in my present circumstances, but from areas of my life that had never been fully healed. The tension, emotional fatigue, irritability, and eventual breakdown of that season were not signs of failure; they were indicators. They revealed that God was inviting me into deeper healing - healing in areas I didn't even realize I needed. My job in that season was not to push harder or manage appearances, but to discern what He was exposing and to allow Him to address it at the root. Healing required my participation, not through striving, but through surrender.

I want to draw your attention to what this participation truly looks like. As established earlier, healing is not just a concept or a process; it is a demonstration of God's power at work. Having already distinguished between authority (*exousia*) and power (*dunamis*) in the previous chapter, we now turn our focus to how that power operates in the work of restoration. Scripture gives us a clear illustration in the account of the woman who touched Jesus:

> *"But Jesus said, 'Someone touched Me, for I perceived that power (dunamis) has gone out from Me.' Then the woman, seeing that she could not go unnoticed, came trembling and fell at His feet. In the presence of all the people, she told why she had touched Him and how she had been instantly healed."* — **Luke 8:46–47 (NIV)**

This encounter reveals healing at the level of *dunamis*; the tangible, life-imparting power of God. What left Jesus entered her, and what entered her immediately restored her. This is the great benefit and expectation we have as believers filled with the Holy Spirit: We have constant access to that exchange of healing; it's not theoretical. It's transferable and experiential, and all it requires is our participation. It's the power of God applied directly to what has been broken throughout the course of our lives.

Healing addresses the aftermath of what we have endured. It tends to the damage left behind by oppression, trauma, loss, sin, heartbreak, injury, and countless other wounds we carry through life. One of the clearest ways to understand healing is this: a wound cannot be restored while the weapon remains embedded within it. What wounds are you still carrying? Where do you still bleed beneath the surface, through impatience, emotional reactivity, withdrawal, or sudden frustration? Pay attention to your responses. The places where you feel easily triggered, short-circuited, defensive, or overwhelmed are often the very places God desires to heal. Deliverance removes the blade. Healing restores the tissue. One addresses what wounded you; the other repairs what was damaged.

Healing may follow deliverance, but it may also follow betrayal, abuse, sickness, grief, or prolonged disappointment. Some wounds are so old they feel indistinguishable from who we are, like childhood memories, fractured relationships, long-standing emotional pain we have learned to live with rather than confront. Yet familiarity does not mean wholeness. Our healing began spiritually at the cross, where Christ secured restoration for every part of our being. But it does not end there. Healing unfolds across time and layers, sometimes instantly, sometimes gradually, as God brings alignment to the spiritual, mental, emotional, and physical dimensions of our lives. What was purchased in full is often received in process, as we allow God to tend carefully to every place that has been wounded.

The assignment of the healing season is participation without interference. Oftentimes, we get in the way of the hard-to-reach areas God intends to heal. Mainly because we don't like the way healing feels when we're in it. This does not mean being passive, though. Healing is not passive, but it is not forced either. Your role in this season is to cooperate with what God is restoring, not to reopen what He is closing, and certainly not to block what He wants access to. This requires trust, discipline, and patience. You must resist the urge to revisit environments, relationships, habits, or thought patterns that God has already removed for the sake of your healing. Healing demands that you believe God at His word, even when the process is uncomfortable, slow, or emotionally demanding.

In this season, you are called to guard what God is healing. That means honoring boundaries He establishes, allowing time to do its work, renewing your mind daily with truth, not rushing back into old patterns and cycles for the sake of keeping busy, and speaking life over areas that still feel tender. You must choose faith over familiarity, obedience over nostalgia, and perseverance over retreat or distraction. Healing is not proven by how quickly the pain leaves, but by how faithfully you remain surrendered while God works beneath the surface. Above all, the assignment of this season is to *let God finish*. Do not rush what He is restoring. Do not shame yourself for needing time. Do not compare your healing to someone else's timeline. Healing belongs to the Lord, and your obedience allows it to take root fully.

Seasons of healing are sacred. They require honesty without condemnation, courage without performance, and faith without guarantees. God does not heal to return you to who you were before the wound. He heals to bring you into who you were always meant to be. When healing is complete, strength replaces fragility, clarity replaces confusion, and peace settles where pain once lived. You are suddenly introduced to a version of yourself you always knew existed, but didn't know how to access. This season prepares you for what comes next and stabilizes you so that future seasons do not reopen old wounds. It teaches you discernment, restraint, and trust. And when healing has done its work, you will discover that what once hurt you no longer controls you. It may be remembered, but it no longer defines you. This is not the end of your process, just the strengthening of it.

Possible Harvests:

- Wholeness
- Emotional clarity
- Renewed faith
- Peace
- Discernment
- Joy not rooted in relief, but in restoration.
- Resilience

PART VI:

Fruit, Stewardship, and Multiplication

Harvest introduces responsibility, not relief.
"Much fruit...so you will be My disciples." — **John 15:8**

The Harvest Season

"Let us not grow weary... for in due season we shall reap." — **Galatians 6:9**

Harvest is a gift, but it is also a test. Harvest is often prayed for, celebrated, and anticipated, but rarely understood. We speak of it as reward, yet Scripture reveals it also as responsibility. Harvest confirms obedience, but it does not replace stewardship. It proves that God is faithful, but it simultaneously tests whether we are.

Many people believe harvest is the *end* of the process, when in reality, it marks the beginning of another. What you receive in harvest reveals not only what you sowed, but whether you are prepared to sustain it. Too often, this realization comes too late, when the increase arrives but the capacity to steward it has not. As a result, many lose the very harvest they labored to produce.

I learned this truth personally in 2024, when I received a lump-sum inheritance I had waited on for more than ten years. When the payout was finally approved, I moved quickly, not with discernment, but with excitement. I made plans immediately, and every plan assumed the harvest was permission rather than responsibility.

I honored God with the first portion. I tithed two thousand dollars and sowed twelve hundred more. But beyond that, my decisions revealed a deeper issue: I knew how to give, but I had not learned how to steward. I spent twelve hundred dollars on a luxury engagement photoshoot, thirteen hundred on a high-end mattress, fifteen hundred to ship my car across the country, five thousand to open a secured credit card, two thousand toward rent, and nineteen hundred on a new sofa. Before I had time to reflect, the harvest was gone.

What I had failed to do was far more costly than what I spent. I saved nothing. I eliminated no debt. I created no strategy to multiply what had been entrusted to me. Within three months, the entire increase was depleted, and I found myself back in a cycle of lack I had once prayed my way out of.

This was not a failure of faith, it was a failure of wisdom. The harvest confirmed that God was faithful, but it also exposed that I was not yet prepared to carry what I had received. Increase had arrived before maturity, and without restraint, it slipped through my hands. I quickly learned harvest does not disappear because God withdraws it; it disappears when stewardship is absent.

Scripture warns us plainly: "From everyone who has been given much, much will be required" (Luke 12:48). This is the weight of stewardship; the sobering truth that without wisdom, increase can be mishandled and what was meant to establish us can be easily fumbled. The harvest only confirms your obedience, not your maturity.

Scripture makes this distinction clear in the story of Cain and Abel. Both men experienced increase as a result of stewardship: Each brought an offering from what had been entrusted to him. Yet it was not the increase itself that determined God's response; it was what they did *after* the increase arrived. Abel's offering reflected reverence and alignment. Cain's revealed immaturity of heart. God's response to Cain was not rejection, but invitation: "If you do what is right, will you not be accepted?" (Genesis 4:7). The issue was never provision, it was posture.

This is where many believers stumble. They assume provision equals approval and increase equals readiness. But Scripture shows us that God often releases harvest before character is fully refined, because harvest responds to seed, not to perfection. Obedience may unlock increase, but wisdom is required to sustain it. What follows the harvest and how it is handled, honored, and stewarded, reveals the true measure of maturity.

Receiving requires wisdom, and there is a grace required to receive well. Some people are disciplined sowers, but careless receivers. They prayed for open doors, yet panic or lose all sense of order and discipline when they swing open. They asked for increase, but collapse under the weight of management, discernment, and restraint. Harvest introduces new decisions, new temptations, and new levels of accountability. What you could pray through in a planting season must now be actionably governed in a harvest season. This is why harvest can feel overwhelming. You are no longer believing for provision; you are responsible for it. No longer is the demand on God to provide, it's on the individual to step into the blessing bestowed upon mankind to "be fruitful, and multiply" what has already been provided.

You'll find that the harvest season does not just reveal fruit; it exposes foundations, and many deep seeded, long hidden things. In seasons of lack, weaknesses can hide. In seasons of abundance, they surface. Harvest does not remove spiritual warfare; it changes its form. Poor boundaries, misaligned priorities, unhealed scarcity, and unmanaged appetites all reveal themselves once increase is present. This is why God does not rush harvest without preparation. He is not withholding, He is protecting you from being crushed by what you asked for.

If the assignment of the planting season was obedience, the assignment of the harvest season is stewardship. You are now responsible to guard, allocate, multiply, and protect what God has released. Harvest must be managed with the same intentionality with which the seed was sown. Otherwise, what was meant to establish you will exhaust you.

Scripture is clear: unguarded harvest spoils.

"Precious treasure and oil are in a wise man's dwelling, but a foolish man devours all he has." — **Proverbs 21:20**

Harvest Is not permission to stop sowing. One of the most dangerous assumptions in harvest season is that sowing is somehow complete. But harvest does not cancel seed, it funds it. Increase is not an exit from faith; it is an invitation to expand it. Those who sustain harvest are those who continue sowing even after breakthrough arrives, because the goal was never just to receive; it was to reproduce.

This season confirms obedience, but it does not suspend discipline. Increase does not remove restraint, it requires it. The same God who trusted you with seed is now watching how you receive the fruit. Harvest is holy ground, and how you step into it matters. The assignment of this season is twofold: to receive with gratitude and to govern with restraint. Gratitude keeps the heart aligned; restraint keeps the harvest protected. Without gratitude, abundance breeds entitlement. Without restraint, blessing becomes consumption. Wisdom is what allows harvest to remain a gift rather than become a burden.

To receive well is to acknowledge the Source without idolizing the supply. To restrain wisely is to enjoy what God has given without exhausting what He entrusted. Harvest is meant to be stewarded, not devoured. Those who pass this test are not just blessed, they are forever established.

"Better is a little with the fear of the Lord than great treasure and trouble with it." — **Proverbs 15:16**

If planting trained your obedience, harvest will refine your wisdom. And when gratitude governs your receiving and restraint guards your increase, God can safely entrust you with fields far beyond what you ever imagined. Those who steward harvest preserve blessing beyond the moment.

Potential Harvest

Harvest produces:

- Provision
- Joy
- Testimony

Seasons of Love

There is so much to be said about love, and so many angles to learn from. However, for the sake of this book and the sanctity of foundations, we will look at love here as the foundational element of every season. Love is not the reward at the end of maturity, it is the environment in which maturity is formed. Every season you walk through is designed to teach you how to love more deeply, more honestly, and more like Christ. But, it starts with receiving His love.

The most important seasons we will ever walk through are seasons of love. Love does not end, diminish, or expire. It is eternal. When we speak of seasons of love, we are not referring to the beginning or ending of love itself, but to the different stages through which God deepens our understanding of it. Love is not static; it matures. And because God is love, growth in Him will always include growth in love; toward Him, toward ourselves, and toward others.

Everything we do is meant to be done in love. Not emotional love. Not conditional love. Not love shaped by wounds, fear, or personal preference. But love as Christ defines it. Scripture makes this clear when Paul prays:

"That your love may abound more and more in knowledge and depth of insight, so that you may discern what is best and may be pure and blameless for the day of Christ." — **Philippians 1:9-10 (AMP)**

Love is meant to increase in depth, not just expression. Seasons of love exist to grow our capacity to love rightly.

Just as God grows our faith through trial and trust, He grows our love through experience and surrender. He is the author and finisher of our faith (Hebrews 12:2), and in the same way, He is the author of love. He teaches us how to love by first showing us how deeply we are loved. And until we learn how to receive His love, we will struggle to give it well. Scripture tells us plainly that without love, everything else is meaningless:

"If I speak in the tongues of men or of angels, but do not have love, I am only a resounding gong or a clanging cymbal... If I have faith that can move mountains, but do not have love, I am nothing." — **1 Corinthians 13:1-2**

Love is not an accessory to spiritual maturity; it is its foundation. So what is love? Love is not a feeling alone, it is a posture. Love is patience, kindness, humility, forgiveness, restraint, endurance, and truth, all flowing from God's love toward us. Love is action. Love is service. Love is self-giving. Scripture defines love not by emotion, but by sacrifice: *"For God so loved the world that He gave..."* (John 3:16).

God's love is revealed in what He gave, not what He felt. And He continues to give, even when we do not deserve it. God is love, and He is our purest example of how love acts and reacts, and yet, many of us struggle here.

When I originally wrote this chapter, I was living through a season of learning love on a deeper level. This was not a chapter I planned to include - not in the first book, and certainly not in the revision. However, it is so necessary to discuss. One day, while washing dishes, the Holy Spirit whispered to me, "Seasons of Love." As I sat with that phrase, I realized that although I had taught love, talked about love, and served in love, I had not fully learned how to receive it.

This season began when the Lord asked me a confronting question: "Why do you reject the love I give you?" I didn't even realize I was doing that, until He showed me a vision of myself building walls. Walls meant to keep pain out, but consequently kept love out, too. I had grown comfortable shutting people out, hiding behind independence and personality, carrying bitterness from past wounds, and calling it strength.

He showed me that walls protect, but they also imprison. I had believed, deep down, that God's love was conditional. That if I sinned, even after repentance, He loved me a little less. That somehow, my mistakes slowly pushed Him further and further away from me. As I write this now, I say it plainly: that belief was wrong.

He knew every failure before I ever made it, and still chose to send Jesus. *"But God demonstrates His own love for us in this: while we were still sinners, Christ died for us."* (Romans 5:8). Love does not withdraw when we fail, instead, love pursues, redeems, and restores. My understanding of love had been shaped by people, not by God. I learned from people that love was earned, withdrawn, conditional, and fragile. But that is not how God loves. Love is not prideful. Love is not easily offended. Love does not keep score. Love is a continual decision to remain faithful regardless of response.

Learning love is learning God, even more, learning how to love how He loves, and it cannot exist outside of relationship. You cannot know someone deeply in a single moment. Rather, you learn them over time. It is the same with God. He desires intimacy that produces growth in Him and understanding of Him, not performance. He wants us to know Him as He is, not as fear, or the world portrays Him. This reality, though, requires deconstruction; deconstruction of old perceptions, patterns, and mindsets regarding love. This is where love steps in as pruning.

The world teaches us that love always says "yes," but God's love sometimes says "no." Scripture tells us: *"Every branch that bears fruit He prunes, so that it will bear even more fruit."* (John 15:2). Pruning is painful, but purposeful. My book, *Wisdom from Eden*, explores this concept deeply in the chapter titled *"The Cutting."* I encourage you to reference it frequently. In summary, God removes what threatens future fruitfulness. For love, this includes mindsets, and worldviews that do not align with His.

I experienced this personally during a season of extreme financial pressure, when my electricity was shut off, my accounts were overdrawn, and every source of dependence was stripped away. I asked a great deal of people, including those who lived in my home freely, and members of my local church at the time for their help financially. All refused. Sadly, the mindset I carried at the time resulted in offense towards them, and anger towards God. I assumed that if something bad were happening to me, it was punishment from God. I went into mental spirals, overanalyzing my every move, wondering what I had done wrong, or what I could have done better to prevent God from being angry with me, and restore peace in my life. What God revealed to me in that season changed everything: The season was not punishment. It was God bringing to the surface that I feared Him, but I didn't love Him.

Scripture teaches us that perfect love casts out fear. (1 John 4:18). I labored for Him because I feared that if I did not, He would punish me. I did not serve out of love, and subsequently, I did not know how to receive it when it came from His hand, because I did not believe His love was sincere. The world had taught me otherwise. That very mindset is what God pruned during that time.

When I finally released fear and my misunderstanding of love - when I finally stopped resisting the pruning, provision came swiftly. Not because God had just arrived, but because I had finally yielded. I stopped demanding from people only what God could give. I tore down the walls that once kept me safe, and received from God what I needed more; His love. That season was never about electricity. It was about love. Tough love. Refining love. Restoring love.

Seasons of giving love soon follow seasons of receiving it. This is where love becomes visible through our lives, especially when it is inconvenient. It looks like loving difficult people, remaining patient with wounded ones, and choosing kindness when offense is available. It was the latter for me. Every person who refused to help me when I was in need, I loved them anyway. I made space to go above and beyond, and continue to love and serve them. I had been filled with the capacity and understanding to do so, so I did. This is discipleship lived out. Jesus was not only a teacher of love, He was its embodiment. He loved through action, sacrifice, endurance, and obedience. And He calls us to do the same. Love is tested in relationship. It is proven under pressure. It is refined through obedience. And it matures across seasons.

The question every season of love asks is simple, yet searching: Do you love conditionally, or do you love as Christ loves you? The assignment of this season is not sentiment, it is transformation. This season calls you to learn how to receive God's love without suspicion, remain in it without shame, and extend it without condition. Love is not proven by what you say, but by how you respond when it costs you something. In this season, you are invited to examine your posture toward love:

1. Do you receive love freely, or brace for it to be taken away?
2. Do you give love generously, or only when it is returned?

3. Do you withdraw when love requires patience, endurance, or forgiveness?

Love is not, and never will be passive. It requires practice. The work of this season is allowing God to dismantle false definitions of love shaped by wounds, rejection, disappointment, fear, or performance, and replace them with His own. This season often includes pruning because God removes pride, control, self-protection, and fear so that love can flow freely and purely. The way you love will be tested, it will be stretched, and it will be refined. But the harvest of this season is undeniable.

When love is allowed to mature, it produces freedom, stability, intimacy, and alignment with the nature of God Himself. Because God is love, every season that teaches you how to love more fully draws you closer to who He is. This is not a season to rush through. This is a season to remain in, until love becomes your reflex.

1 Corinthians 13 & The Love Challenge

Use the questions below as a mirror, not a measure. Return to them often.

Am I patient?

Am I kind?

Am I not envious or jealous?

Am I not prideful?
Am I considerate?
Am I selfless?
Am I not easily angered?
Am I forgiving?
Do I rejoice in truth?
Am I hopeful?
Am I faithful?

If you discovered areas that need growth, do not be discouraged. Awareness is grace. God reveals what He intends to heal. When you sow love, you reap love, along with joy, peace, patience, kindness, goodness, faithfulness, gentleness, and self-control. Above all, you reap Christ's very character, and *that* is the harvest of this season.

The Governing Season

And the Lord said, "Who then is that faithful and wise steward, whom his Lord shall make ruler over his household, to give them their portion of food at the proper time? — **Luke 12:42**

Of the many seasons we've discussed, I believe the governing season is most where leaders are discovered and developed. This season will expose your readiness for leadership. The Governing Season is not loud. It does not announce itself with celebration or acceleration. This is the season where fruit no longer belongs solely to you. It is the transition from personal obedience to shared responsibility, from producing fruit to preserving it. Many know how to bear fruit, but few know how to keep it. Jesus makes this distinction clear when He says, "I chose you and appointed you that you should go and bear fruit, and that your fruit should remain" (John 15:16). Bearing fruit requires obedience;

keeping fruit requires wisdom. The Governing Season begins when God entrusts you not only with increase, but with oversight.

Governance introduces submitted authority without urgency. Earlier seasons demanded swift obedience and decisive movement, but this season requires patience and restraint. Scripture tells us that "a king will reign in righteousness, and princes will rule with justice" (Isaiah 32:1). Righteous rule is measured, prayerful, and forward-seeing. Those who govern well do not confuse momentum with mandate or activity with assignment. They understand that all "doing" does not equate to productivity, and all "work" is not God's work. They understand that what is built too quickly is rarely sustained. In this season, God often slows your pace while expanding your influence, teaching you that wisdom governs speed.

This season also shifts your vision beyond yourself. Governance asks a sobering question: what must remain after you are no longer present? Proverbs reminds us that "a good man leaves an inheritance to his children's children" (Proverbs 13:22). Inheritance is not limited to finances; it includes systems, values, spiritual order, culture, and covering. The Governing Season requires generational thinking. God begins to move you from being a participant to custodian, from a builder to keeper. You are no longer preparing for what God will do next; you are preserving what He has already done.

Governance always involves people. Scripture teaches that "whoever is faithful in very little is faithful also in much" (Luke 16:10). In this season, "much" often looks like responsibility for others' outcomes, decisions that affect more than yourself, and influence that carries consequence. Authority is no longer theoretical; it becomes relational. God entrusts people, resources, and responsibility to those who understand that authority is stewardship, not ownership. People are not possessions, and influence is not entitlement. You are accountable not only for what you produce, but for how others flourish under your care.

One of the greatest dangers of the Governing Season is independence. Experience can quietly replace dependence if the heart is not guarded. Scripture warns us, "Not by might nor by power, but by My Spirit, says the Lord" (Zechariah 4:6). Those who govern well remain deeply submitted to God. They pray before deciding, listen before leading, and submit before directing. Governance sustained apart from the Spirit eventually collapses under its own weight. True authority remains anchored in humility.

This is also why the Governing Season is often quiet. There is little applause here. Much of the work happens behind the scenes through structuring, guarding, discerning, maintaining, and protecting. This is not the season of display; it is the season of preservation. Scripture reminds us that "it is required in stewards that one be found faithful" (1 Corinthians 4:2). Faithfulness, not visibility, is the measure of success in this season.

The assignment of this season is to conduct a stewardship and oversight inventory before God. Set aside intentional time to examine what has been entrusted to you in this season, including relationships, resources, influence, platforms, and responsibility. Ask where you are reacting instead of governing, and what areas lack structure, protection, or sustainability. Consider which decisions you may be delaying out of discomfort rather than discernment, and what would suffer if you stepped away tomorrow, as this directly points to what was built in your own strength. Be honest, and invite the Holy Spirit to reveal where order, boundaries, or recalibration are needed.

Potential Harvest

- Sustained fruit
- Increased trust from God
- Clear, peaceful decision-making
- Enduring legacy

The Maintenance Season

"It is required of stewards that one be found faithful."
— 1 Corinthians 4:2

While the governing season decides what should exist and how it should be ordered, the maintenance season sustains what has *already* been decided and ordered. Governance sets the direction. Maintenance preserves the function. The maintenance season is often overlooked because it does not come with visible markers of progress. There are no dramatic breakthroughs, no sudden shifts, no obvious rewards. Yet this season is just as sacred as planting, harvest, or transition, because it determines whether what God has built will last. Not every season expands, some preserve. Not every assignment excites, some sustain. It is through maintenance where longevity is decided.

This season teaches consistency without excitement. It requires discipline without applause. It calls for attentiveness when momentum slows and faithfulness when results are absent. Many people mistake this season for stagnation, and punish themselves for what seems to be disconnection from God. But silence here does not mean God has withdrawn, nor does it mean you have done anything wrong. Often, it means He is watching how you care for what He has already entrusted to you.

I encountered this season most clearly while writing and publishing my first two books. There was momentum leading up to their release; long nights of writing, revelation flowing freely, and the deep satisfaction of obedience fulfilled. *A Harvest for Every Season* was completed. *Wisdom from Eden* followed four years later. I felt accomplished. The assignment had been completed. And then there was silence.

After publication, fewer than two hundred copies sold between both books. There was no surge. No increase. No affirmation from the outside. God did not speak again about the outcome. Yet I knew with certainty that I had heard Him clearly at the beginning. I knew He told me to write those books. I also knew He had promised increase through them.

The test, however, was not whether I could complete the project. The test was whether I would remain faithful to what had been produced once momentum disappeared and God seemed quiet. Would I maintain alignment with what He had spoken when there was no visible evidence of fulfillment? This is where many abandon their calling, not because they lack obedience, but because they misunderstand silence. God's silence did not mean His promise had changed. It meant my posture was being examined.

Maintenance seasons expose whether obedience was outcome-driven or covenant-anchored. They reveal whether we serve the promise, or the God who made it. So, I did the only thing I knew to do: I kept writing. I kept publishing. Not because the outcome was rewarding, but because obedience still mattered. Scripture tells us, "You have been faithful over little; I will set you over much" (Matthew 25:21). I believe this includes faithfulness over silence. Faithfulness when nothing is moving. Faithfulness when no one is watching.

The question was never whether I knew what was right. I know the wisdom God has entrusted to me. I know who He has called me to be. The real question was whether I would remain that person without applause; whether I would keep the same posture when God was not visibly promoting or highlighting what He had once promised. That is the work of the maintenance season.

This season exists to preserve what was built in previous ones. What you planted must be tended. What you harvested must be guarded. Without maintenance, growth becomes unstable. And as we discuss in the chapter, *Seasons of Pruning*, expansion without preservation eventually collapses under its own weight.

Scripture does not say it is required of stewards that they be impressive, innovative, or fast. It says they must be faithful. Faithfulness looks like consistency in prayer, integrity in finances, discipline in routine, and attentiveness to small things that protect what God has already established.

The assignment of the maintenance season is clear: remain attentive, faithful, and disciplined.

1. Remain attentive so small breaches do not become silent erosion.
2. Remain faithful so consistency does not give way to complacency.
3. Remain disciplined so what God built through your hands is not undone in quiet neglect.

Maintenance does not, and may not ever feel like progress, but it is preparation. It prepares what God has built to carry abundance without collapsing under it. Those who honor this season are often the ones God later trusts with increase, not because they chased expansion, but because they proved they could sustain what already existed, with or without applause.

The maintenance season will not announce itself as important. It will feel ordinary. Repetitive. Easily overlooked. It often looks like faithful labor with no visible return, obedience without recognition, and/or consistency without confirmation. Yet, this is where foundations are reinforced and collapse of all you've built is quietly prevented. Nothing may appear to be changing on the surface, but everything is being strengthened beneath it.

Faithfulness does not need volume to carry weight. It is powerful because it is proven, and it is never unseen by God. Those who honor maintenance do not spend future seasons repairing what should have been preserved. What is protected in quiet seasons does not have to be rebuilt through loss. This is the strength of stewardship, and it is why God entrusts increase to those who remain faithful when no one is watching.

Potential Harvest

Maintenance produces:

- Longevity
- Protection from loss
- Stability

The Multiplication Season

"You did not choose Me... I appointed you that you should go and bear fruit, and that your fruit should remain." — **John 15:16**

Multiplication is not simply increase, it's entrustment, and harvest with responsibility. This season arrives when God determines that what has been built can now extend beyond you without losing its integrity. Your harvest becomes legacy, your fruit becomes supply, and your obedience shifts from personal faithfulness to communal responsibility. This is why multiplication feels heavier than harvest. While harvest confirms obedience, multiplication confirms trust.

Jesus makes a critical distinction in John 15: fruit is not only meant to appear, it is meant to remain. Temporary success is not the goal of the Kingdom; sustainable fruit is. Multiplication is not about producing more, but about producing fruit that can nourish others without rotting under pressure. In this season, God is no longer asking, Can you carry it? He is asking, Can others eat from it safely?

Consider what it feels like to walk into a grocery store expecting nourishment, only to find bruised, spoiled, or rotting fruit on the shelves. Even if the store is full, you leave disappointed because you understand abundance without quality is not provision. No one wants to be sold something that looks available but is unsafe for consumption.

In the same way, God does not multiply fruit so it can be offered prematurely, carelessly, or in a damaged state. Fruit that feeds others must be handled with care. It must be clean, mature, and distributed with discernment. To give spoiled harvest in the name of generosity is not kindness, it is negligence. What is meant to bless must first be refined enough to sustain. Multiplication, then, is not just about availability, it's about responsibility. God is not interested in increasing output if the fruit cannot nourish without harm. What He multiplies must be worthy of those it is meant to serve.

This is likely why some projects you rushed to start and finish never spread, and why certain messages, music, or teachings you released did not reach the masses you expected. The grace of God will often allow us to produce, but His mercy will restrain our reach when expansion would cause more harm than good. God is too faithful to amplify what has not yet been fully refined. Thus, silence is not always rejection, it's protection. He will not multiply fruit that could bruise those it is meant to bless.

What was produced in obedience may still require maturity before it is trusted with influence. And what feels like delay is often God safeguarding both the receiver and the steward. Reach is not withheld because God is unwilling; it is delayed because He is responsible.

While planting seasons tend to focus inward on obedience, surrender, formation, and maintenance seasons stabilize what has been built, multiplication seasons turn outward, and shift the focus from you to others. This is where many become disoriented. Increase now comes with demand. People look to you for wisdom, covering, provision, leadership, and example. What once sustained you must now sustain others. And not everyone who celebrates your fruit is meant to access it.

Multiplication requires discernment, not just generosity. Fruit is meant to feed others, but not to be wasted, mishandled, or prematurely given away.

> *"A wise man saves for the future, but the foolish man spends whatever he gets."* — **Proverbs 21:20**

This is where many falter: Multiplication without discernment leads to depletion. They confuse multiplication with availability, and begin to pour without boundaries, give without wisdom, and distribute without prayer. What God multiplied to establish them becomes the very thing that exhausts them. They misunderstand that multiplication does not mean everyone gets access. It means God assigns you responsibility over increase, but wisdom determines who, when, and how fruit is shared.

In this season, you're entering into a space that requires more than faith alone. Faith carried you through planting, discipline sustained you through maintenance, but multiplication requires leadership, and leadership means structure. It means systems. It means knowing what scales and what must remain protected. God multiplies what can be governed. This is why Jesus did not disciple crowds, He discipled twelve. Even in multiplication, He was selective, because He understood fruit that remains must be stewarded intentionally.

The assignment of this season is clear: pour into others with wisdom and discernment. Pour without ego. Pour without depletion. Pour without abandoning order Remain rooted in obedience. Continue sowing even while fruit is multiplying. Guard your posture as carefully as your provision. Multiplication is not permission to relax. Instead, it is a call to maturity.

"The fruit of the righteous is a tree of life, and whoever captures souls is wise." — **Proverbs 11:30**

When God multiplies your fruit, He is not simply increasing your reach, He is extending His provision through you. And when you steward this season well, the fruit does not just grow, it remains.

Potential Harvest

This season produces:

- Legacy
- Generational impact
- Influence beyond self

PART VII:

Completion & Commissioning

Every completed season releases you into the next assignment. *"He who began a good work...will complete it."*
— **Philippians 1:6**

The Completion / Transition Season

"The end of a matter is better than its beginning."
— **Ecclesiastes 7:8**

Of all the seasons we've discussed, seasons of completion and transition often hit the hardest. I group these two together because, though they differ in expression, they both usher in new beginnings. We tend to resist endings because we misinterpret them, assuming closure means failure, loss, or regression. But Scripture reveals something far more sacred: completion is not collapse; it is fulfillment. What God completes, He does not abandon. He concludes it with intention, so that what comes next can be received whole. Endings are holy. Completion prepares the heart for new beginnings.

An ending does not mean something went wrong. Often, it means something went right - you saw a thing through from start to finish, beginning, middle, and end.

Completion seasons are holy because they seal what was built, taught, endured, and stewarded. They mark the point where grace carried you as far as it was meant to, and no further. To linger beyond completion is not faithfulness; it is disobedience disguised as loyalty.

I encountered this unsettling reality in a deeply personal way when my season as a single mother came to an abrupt end. When I became engaged to my now husband, what should have felt like celebration was accompanied by grief. I mourned more than a relationship status. I grieved my entire identity. Who I was, everything I had become, slowly started to fade away as new roles and responsibilities assumed their position.

For most of my life, independence had been my survival. My business, my decision-making, my pace, my authority over my own life, all of it had been shaped in a season where I carried everything alone. And suddenly, that chapter was closing. I interpreted the transition as loss. Loss of independence. Loss of identity. Loss of the version of myself that had learned how to endure without help. Even though I explore this transition in greater depth in my next book, it is important to say here: that ending was not punishment. It was holy. What I was losing was not who I was, it was who I no longer needed to be.

Completion seasons, like many others, can feel like loss. They are often uncomfortable because they dismantle what once worked. But God does not destroy what He completes, He fulfills it. The skills, strength, discipline, and wisdom I gained as a single mother were not erased; they were integrated. That season ended not because it failed, but because it succeeded and prepared me for what came next: becoming a wife who could receive her husband's support in business, a wife who had already learned the skills needed to help build what God had entrusted to them together, and a mother who no longer had to carry the full weight of parenthood alone.

The danger in completion seasons is not the ending itself, it is mislabeling the ending as loss rather than transition. When we call holy closure "failure," we grieve incorrectly. And unresolved grief hardens the heart against what God is trying to birth next. I had to learn how not to sink into depression over what was ending, but instead discern what was being completed, and what God was currently birthing.

One of the greatest lessons of this season was understanding that I could not enter the new thing broken. I had to enter it whole. But wholeness required release. I had to release my former life with gratitude, not resentment. Trust, not fear. Honor, not nostalgia. Completion demanded that I bless what was ending rather than cling to it for the sake of identity or comfort. This is the quiet work of transition seasons: learning how to let go without falling apart.

> *"Remember not the former things, nor consider the things of old. Behold, I am doing a new thing..."* — **Isaiah 43:18-19**

God does new things after closure, not during confusion. New beginnings require cleared ground. Not scorched earth, but cleared soil.

The assignment of this season is simple, but sacred: release with gratitude and trust. Gratitude acknowledges that the last season served its purpose. Trust affirms that God is faithful beyond what you can see next. Together, they prevent you from carrying old versions of yourself into places they no longer belong. You are not dishonoring the past by releasing it. You are honoring God by recognizing His timing.

Completion seasons cause transition seasons, and prepare the heart to receive, not as a wounded version of who you were, but as a whole and ready version of who you are becoming. Remember, endings are holy, and completion is not failure, it is fulfillment of a season. And when you release what God has finished, you make room for the fullness of what He is about to begin. Isaiah 43:18–19 reminds us that God does new things after closure. Those who honor endings enter new seasons whole.

Potential Harvest

Transition produces:

- Peace
- Emotional closure
- Readiness for the next season

A Harvest for Every Season

"The sower sows the word." — **Mark 4:14**

Life is lived in seedtime and harvest, continually. Not once. Not in isolated moments. But in an ongoing rhythm that governs every area of growth, healing, and transformation. Scripture is clear: "As long as the earth endures, seedtime and harvest...will never cease" (Genesis 8:22). That means there is never a season where this principle is suspended. What changes is not the rhythm, but our willingness to remain in it.

Most people do not fail because the harvest is impossible. They fail because they abandon the process when the harvest is not immediate. We quit when results take longer than expected. We disengage when progress is invisible. We grow weary when resolve is delayed. Whether it is believing for maturity in a spouse, healing in the body, freedom from exhausting sin, mental resilience, weight loss or restoration, emotional wholeness, or even something as practical as growing stronger hair or a healthier routine, the pattern is always the same. There is seedtime. There is growth. And there is harvest. Always.

The mistake is assuming that harvest only counts when it looks dramatic. In reality, we are sowing and reaping simultaneously across different areas of our lives at all times. While one area is in seedtime, another is in harvest. While one discipline feels slow, another is bearing fruit. God is not linear in His work within us, but He is faithful in His order. When we continue to sow, we are never idle. When we remain consistent, we are never behind, so endure! What guarantees harvest is not your intensity, it's your endurance. Remember, scripture warns us plainly: "Let us not grow weary in doing good, for at the proper time we will reap a harvest if we do not give up" (Galatians 6:9). The condition of the promise is not perfection. It is persistence. Your harvest is assured not by your talent, gifting, or even passion, but by your refusal to abandon what God has already instructed you to do.

This is where many misunderstand timing. We want a singular harvest moment, but God works through continual harvest seasons. There is always a now harvest available for what was previously sown. And there is always a next harvest being prepared by what you are sowing today. In the same way, there is always a seed you can plant now, and always another one that will follow.

Growth seasons feel slow because roots are forming. Maintenance seasons feel quiet because foundations are being strengthened. Multiplication seasons feel heavy because responsibility increases. But none of these seasons are wasted, and none of them are optional. You do not bypass seedtime to get to harvest, you pass through it, and the only way to guarantee that you will *not* reap is to quit.

Those who endure learn a different kind of faith, not faith that chases outcomes, but faith that trusts process. They understand that God is faithful to His word, even when progress is imperceptible. They know that harvest is not delayed, it is layered, and that every act of obedience is contributing to something that will eventually surface. Life is seedtime and harvest, again and again. And the ones who reap are not the ones who rush, they are the ones who remain.

Your life is meant to be experienced, not rushed through or reduced to outcomes alone. We are here for a short while, which is why Scripture urges us to live with spiritual awareness, looking not only at what is seen, but at what is unseen. Fruitfulness always begins where the eye cannot yet reach. Before anything manifests naturally, it is first cultivated spiritually.

To reap a spiritual harvest is to be entrusted with the capacity to reap a natural one. When God forms something in the spirit, He is preparing it to eventually take shape in the world around you. This is why it is worth pausing to reflect on each season we have discussed so far. What do you see now that you could not see then? Each season carried its own harvest, but not one of them was measured by what the five senses could detect. Their true yield was internal.

If you look back, you will see every season harvested something in the spirit. Love was formed through endurance, joy through surrender, peace through trust, patience through delay, kindness through compassion, goodness through obedience, faithfulness through consistency, gentleness through humility, and self-control through restraint. The fruit of the Spirit was not produced all at once, but cultivated gradually, across seasons, simply by living your life and faithfully walking through what came your way. You have been reaping all along.

Now, the invitation is to learn how to sow what you have already harvested spiritually so that it may produce a natural harvest, one that blesses you, blesses others, and brings glory to our Father in heaven. Spiritual fruit is not meant to remain abstract. It is meant to take form, create impact, and establish life.

So, my dear friends, let us not grow weary in doing good. If you are going through, you are growing through. There is a harvest for every season you face, and there is fruit available to be gathered, right now. There is a harvest for every season, and the ones who endure will always return rejoicing. Run out and reap your harvest!

> *"LORD, make us prosperous again, just as the rain brings water back to dry riverbeds. Let those who wept as they sowed their seed gather the harvest with joy. Those who wept as they went carrying the seed will come back singing for joy, as they bring in the harvest."*
> **— Psalm 126:4-6 (GNB)**

About the Author

Raven Makenzie is a faith-based life coach, author, and mentor devoted to helping individuals navigate seasons of transition with clarity, peace, and spiritual alignment.

Known for her grounded teaching and discerning voice, Raven specializes in guiding people who feel "in between," those who sense God is doing something new but are unsure how to move without striving or fear. Her work bridges Scripture, personal formation, and practical wisdom, equipping readers and clients to recognize God's timing and respond with obedience rather than anxiety.

Raven's writing and coaching emphasize identity, discernment, and spiritual maturity, encouraging believers to trust the process of becoming and the faithfulness of God in every season.

She is the founder of the Raven Makenzie brand and the creator of transformational coaching frameworks centered on alignment, authority, and peace.

"Let us not grow weary while doing good, for in due season we shall reap if we do not lose heart."

— **Galatians 6:9**

www.ingramcontent.com/pod-product-compliance
Lightning Source LLC
Chambersburg PA
CBHW050908160426
43194CB00011B/2323